Communications in Computer and Information Science 1554

More information about this series at https://link.springer.com/bookseries/7899

Shiva Raj Pokhrel · Min Yu · Gang Li (Eds.)

Applications and Techniques in Information Security

12th International Conference, ATIS 2021
Virtual Event, December 16–17, 2021
Revised Selected Papers

 Springer

Editors
Shiva Raj Pokhrel (iD)
Deakin University
Burwood, Australia

Min Yu (iD)
Chinese Academy of Sciences
Beijing, China

Gang Li (iD)
Deakin University
Burwood, Australia

ISSN 1865-0929 ISSN 1865-0937 (electronic)
Communications in Computer and Information Science
ISBN 978-981-19-1165-1 ISBN 978-981-19-1166-8 (eBook)
https://doi.org/10.1007/978-981-19-1166-8

This Springer imprint is published by the registered company Springer Nature Singapore Pte Ltd.
The registered company address is: 152 Beach Road, #21-01/04 Gateway East, Singapore 189721, Singapore

Preface

The 2021 International Conference on Applications and Technologies in Information Security (ATIS 2021) was the 12th event in the ATIS series, which started in 2010. The purpose of ATIS is to provide a forum for presentation and discussion of innovative ideas, research results, applications, and experience from around the world. The annual ATIS conference highlights new results in the design and analysis of digital security hardware and software implementations. ATIS provides a valuable connection between the theoretical and implementation communities and attracts participants from industry, academia, and government organizations.

As academic research in information security has developed over the last twenty or so years, applications and techniques are being developed to be of specific use in this area. These include wavelets and their applications in digital forensics, classification algorithms for use in malicious software detection, and genetic algorithms custom-made for the cryptographic community, etc.

ATIS 2021 focused on all aspects of new theories, novel techniques, and innovative applications of Cybersecurity, Zero Trust Access (ZTA) Architecture, and Privacy/Security of Autonomous Vehicles. The increasing trends towards remote working, working from home, and distributed collaboration have challenged previously established security and privacy notions, particularly the perimeter-based security architecture. This ensuing trend has driven the need for a radical redesign of the security architectures and has already led to the emergence of new concepts such as ZTA. In contrast to the existing security notions, ZTA aims to think about security in a new philosophical way—to continuously verify every user and every device before granting access to a network or an asset.

Our major focus in ATIS 2021 was to uncover the dynamics of the vulnerabilities posed by new enterprise demands such as bring your own device (BYOD) including others, and develop new insights that requires novel approaches and advances towards more intelligent, agile and adaptable framework so as to a constantly cope with the evolving threat landscape. ATIS 2021 received a total of 57 papers, of which 16 were accepted. All submitted papers followed a double-blind review policy. On average, each paper received six peer reviews.

January 2022   Shiva Raj Pokhrel

Organization

General Chair

Robin Doss   Deakin University, Australia
Hai L. Vu   Monash University, Australia

Program Committee Chair

Shiva Raj Pokhrel   Deakin University, Australia

Steering Committee

Lynn Batten   Deakin University, Australia
Robin Doss   Deakin University, Australia
Heejo Lee   Korea University, South Korea
Gang Li   Deakin University, Australia
Jiqiang Liu   Beijing Jiaotong University, China
Tsutomu Matsumoto   Yokohama National University, Japan
Wenjia Niu   Chinese Academy of Sciences, China
Shiva Raj Pokhrel   Deakin University, Australia
Bheemarjuna Reddy Tamma   Indian Institute of Technology (IIT) Hyderabad,
                                           India
Hai L. Vu   Monash University, Australia
Min Yu   Chinese Academy of Sciences, China
Yuliang Zheng   University of Alabama at Birmingham, USA

Program Committee

Samman Bhattarai   Charles Sturt University, Australia
Yang Cao   Deakin University, Australia
Ramji Chalise   Knox City Council, Australia
Antony Franklin   Indian Institute of Technology (IIT) Hyderabad,
                                           India
Mohammad Belayet Hossain   Deakin University, Australia
Niranjan Khakurel   Pokhara University, Nepal
Abhinav Kumar   Indian Institute of Technology (IIT) Hyderabad,
                                           India
Muhammad Baqer Mollah   Nanyang Technology University, Singapore
Bahaa Al-Musawi   University of Kufa, Iraq

James Elliot Nemecek	Deakin University, Australia
Sashi Raj Pandey	Kyung Hee University, South Korea
Sebastian Alarcon Pinto	DXC Consulting, Australia
Parshu Pokhrel	Herbert Smith Freehills, Australia
Shiva Raj Pokhrel	Deakin University, Australia
Shyam Kumar Shrestha	Fisher & Paykel Healthcare, Australia
Surmarga Kumar Sah Tyagi	Zhongyuan University of Technology, China
Bheemarjuna Reddy Tamma	Indian Institute of Technology (IIT) Hyderabad, India
Shashank Vatedka	Indian Institute of Technology (IIT) Hyderabad, India
Sandeep Verma	Dr. B R Ambedkar National Institute of Technology, India
Rongxin Xu	Hunan University, China
Zhenshuai Xu	Jilin University, China
Min Yu	Chinese Academy of Sciences, China

Additional Reviewers

Ziwei Hou	Deakin University, Australia
Yishuo Zhang	Deakin University, Australia
Xiaojuan Cheng	Deakin University, Australia
Shu Li	Deakin University, Australia
Mengyue Deng	Hunan University, China
Yang Cao	Deakin University, Australia
Xin Han	Xi'an Shiyou University, China
Haiyang Xia	Australian National University, Australia

Contents

Cloud and IoT

Communication and Data Mining

Machine Learning

Prediction of the Water Cut with the Hybrid Optimized SVR

Shaowei Pan$^{(\boxtimes)}$ ⓘ, Yuhui Mou ⓘ, and Zechen Zheng ⓘ

Xi'an Shiyou University, Xi'an 710065, Shaanxi, China

Abstract. The moisture content identification of a water drive oilfield is related to how to formulate and adjust the development plan of the oil field. However, traditional prediction methods for the water cut usually have problems such as slow recognition speed and limited by the specific conditions of the oil well. Therefore, in order to avoid the influence of the above problems, a machine algorithm model of water cut based on hybrid optimization is proposed, which is based on the support vector regression (SVR) model. First, the data is constructed by time sliding window; secondly, on the basis of the fundamental SVR model, this paper combines the Particle Swarm Optimization (PSO) and the Artificial Fish Swarm Algorithm (AFSA) to optimize the hyperparameters of the SVR prediction model to achieve better experimental results; finally, if the hybrid model proposed in this article has some good experimental results, then it can be applied to the actual water cut prediction of the oilfield. After comparing four different models, the prediction model based on the hybrid optimization algorithm proposed in this paper has some good experimental results. The prediction curve and the real curve have the same trend as a whole, and the subtle errors are also the smallest. Thus, it performs better than the SVR prediction model optimized by the differential evolution algorithm, the SVR prediction model optimized by the genetic algorithm, and the SVR prediction model optimized by the PSO.

Keywords: Water cut identification · Particle swarm optimization algorithm · Artificial Fish Swarm Algorithm · SVR · Prediction

1 Introduction

At present, a lot of water injection oilfields have entered into a middle or high water cut level, therefore, whether the water cut can be accurately predicted is of great significance to the formulation of water drive oilfield development plans [1, 2]. For this reason, many scholars, engineers and technicians have carried out the research in this area. Nowadays, there are three main existing water cut prediction methods, namely, the mathematical model [3] method, the water drive characteristic curve method [3], and the machine learning method [4].

Each of the above methods has certain shortcomings: For example, traditional method the water drive characteristic curve method can only reflect the connection between the degree of harvest cut and the moisture content, it cannot predict the time of oilfield

© Springer Nature Singapore Pte Ltd. 2022
S. R. Pokhrel et al. (Eds.): ATIS 2021, CCIS 1554, pp. 3–12, 2022.
https://doi.org/10.1007/978-981-19-1166-8_1

development and the change law of moisture content, it has such flaws; The mathematical model lacks a certain seepage theory, so there are many difficulties in directly applying the mathematical model to specific oil well experiments. Therefore, the method of using the mathematical model to predict the water cut has certain defects.

Support vector regression algorithm, as a kind of machine learning method, has a strict mathematical support and a short training time, and it due to the statistical theory. Besides, it is a concrete implementation structure of the consistency principle for the structural risk minimization. However, when we apply the SVR model to actual engineering problems, there will be some unavoidable problems in the SVR model, that is, the parameters that affect the performance of the algorithm cannot be accurately selected, which leads to the uncertainty of the accuracy of the model. Therefore, the genetic algorithm [5], the PSO [6] and the AFSA [7] are used to optimize the Support Vector Machine (SVM), so as to avoid the influence of the uncertain parameters on moisture content prediction. The non-linear characteristics of the support vector regression machine can make the model adapt to the complicated and the changeable water cut of oilfield, and can basically avoid the uncertain influence of the reservoir factors. Therefore, the SVR model based on the differential evolution algorithm, the SVR model based on the genetic algorithm, the SVR model based on the PSO and the SVR model based on the PSO - AFSA are compared. Finally, this paper compares the prediction results of the above four models for moisture content, and selects the model with the highest prediction accuracy according to the evaluation criteria.

2   Related Works

The characteristic curve method of water drive is a classic method in this field to predict water cut, and it has been widely used by many researchers. In addition, many researchers have applied some mathematical models from the economics and the statistics to the water cut prediction. These models mainly include the Logistic model [8], the Goempertz model [9] and the Usher model [10]. Nowadays, with the continuous development of machine learning, it has gradually begun to play an important role in various industries applications [11], and it is also used in water cut prediction.

In this field, a classic method is called the water drive characteristic curve method. Someone previously used this method to predict the moisture content of the oil field. However, this method also has its own shortcomings. Using this method can only reflect the connection between the moisture content and the degree of collection, in the actual field of petroleum engineering, it cannot predict the change law of moisture content and the time of oilfield development [12]. And these mathematical models are based on other disciplines, the physical connotation of the parameters is unclear and the seepage theory is lacking in these models. Besides, there are many differences between different oil wells and different oilfields. As a result, there are many difficulties when applying these mathematical models directly to specific oil wells. When long short-term memory (LSTM) [4] is used to forecast the moisture content, the LSTM model also has certain shortcomings, for example, it is hard to find the suitable parameters of the model, lots of training data is required, and it takes long time to train model. SVR model also has the problem that it is difficult to select the suitable configuration parameters. However, compared with LSTM, SVR requires fewer data samples and shorter time during training, so it is very convenient to optimize the parameters. Besides, it has a strong interpretability. Therefore, SVR has been chosen as the basic model to be optimized in this paper.

In order to acquire a relatively accurate water cut prediction model, this essay uses the differential evolution algorithm, the genetic algorithm, the PSO and the PSO - AFSA to optimize the parameters of the SVR. After optimization, the model that finds the appropriate parameters is applied to the water content prediction experiment.

3 Methodology

3.1 SVR

In the 1970s, Vapnik proposed the SVM [13] model, which utilizes the VC Dimension (Vapnik-Chervonenkis Dimension) theory of the theoretical knowledge of statistics. The SVM model follows the principle of the structural risk minimization and has strong generalization performance on samples, thus it can avoid the high dependence on sample data. When the SVM model is applied to the field of nonlinear regression prediction, it is called the SVR model. In simple terms, SVM is to find a flat in the known data distribution space. This flat can make the two types of data the farthest distance from this flat to achieve the purpose of classifying the data set. While the SVR regression is to find a regression flat in the space composed of all data. This flat can be that all the data in the data space have the closest distance to this plane. The SVR regression model creates an isolation on both sides of the linear function. If there are data samples in this isolation, the data in the data band will not count the loss function; on the contrary, the data samples outside the isolation will count the loss function. Finally, the SVR regression model is optimized by reducing the overall width of the isolation zone and the overall loss function value.

3.2 PSO

Humans design algorithms by observing the behavior of animals. For example, PSO is an algorithm designed to simulate a flock of birds looking for food. Eberhart and Kennedy proposed this algorithm in 1995 [14]. Suppose all the solutions of the problem are a bird, and call them particles in the algorithm. Among them, an artificially set appropriate value function is needed, and the counted value is used to judge the movement of the particles. Each particle has a site and speed. The speed will determine the distance and direction the particles fly. Each particle will count its own fitness value according to a given fitness function, and update its site and speed according to the site and speed update formula. Then iterate over and over again to find the optimal solution in the space.

3.3 AFSA

Li Xiaolei designed a new algorithm to simulate the behavior of a school of fish, this algorithm is called AFSA [15] in 2002. Three basal behaviors of fish were used to improve the algorithm: the follow behavior, the swarm behavior and the prey behavior.

Each artificial fish in the fish school can achieve local optimization, so that the global optimal can be displayed in the whole and the crowd.

Follow behavior: When the objective function calculation result of the optimal site in the solution space is better than the objective function calculation result of the current place, and the area near the site is very little, the fish at that site will dolly one step toward the optimal fish school site, otherwise the fish school will simulate predation actions. Swarm behavior: The fish in the school counts the number of fish near the current site and counts their center site. Then the objective function calculation result of the new center site and the objective function calculation result of the current site were compared. If the newly obtained objective function calculation result of the center site is better than the objective function calculation result of the current site, and the number of fish around the site is not much. The artificial fish dolly one step from current site to the center site, otherwise the artificial fish will simulate predation. Prey behavior: First set a state for the artificial fish, and then stochastically select another state within the range it can perceive. If the calculation result of the objective function in the new state is better than the calculation result of the objective function in the current state, then the artificial fish will go forward to the new state, otherwise a state is stochastically selected again. When the number of selected states reaches a given number, but the calculation result of the objective function still does not meet the set conditions, the artificial fish will dolly one step stochastically.

3.4 PSO-AFSA-SVR

Since particle swarm optimization algorithm only relies on the speed of the particles to complete the search, and it lacks the dynamic adjustment of the speed, so it is common to get the local solution in solution space, lead to low convergence accuracy or difficulty in convergence. Therefore, this characteristic may affect the quality of the model. The PSO is used to find the optimal hyperparameter interval of the prediction model of SVR in a larger range, so that the initialization population will inevitably have a good optimization result. And then the artificial fish population of the AFSA is initialized in this hyperparameter optimization interval. Since AFSA has the significant characteristic of jumping out of local optimal calculation result, the algorithm can optimize the experimental consequent of PSO in a small range, further optimize the consequent of PSO, and achieve the purpose of deviating from the local optimal solution found by the algorithm. Therefore, it can outcrop the suitable parameters that may exist in the adjacent interval. The chart of the PSO-AFSA-SVR algorithm is Fig. 1. In Fig. 1, X and V are the site and the velocity of each particle respectively, N is the number of times of iterations in the calculation process and Maxiter is the maximum number of iterations. The implication of C, ε and γ is that C is the penalty factor, ε is the insensitive loss coefficient and γ is the parameter of RBF kernel function.

Specific steps of the PSO-AFSA-SVR algorithm are in follows:

(1) First set the size of the particle swarm and the maximum number of iterations *iter*, then initialize the velocity and site of the particle swarm;
(2) Next, count the fitness of each particle in the artificially set particle swarm, and the fitness function is given artificially;

(3) Next, the fitness of each particle is compared with the historical best fitness of each particle, and the fitness of each particle is compared with the fitness of the global best site, and then the best individual historical site and the best global site of each particle are updated;

(4) After meeting the termination conditions, output the best optimization parameters of the PSO optimization algorithm;

(5) Set the size of artificial fish schools N, the maximum number of iterations *iter*, the step *Step*, the visual *visual*, the maximum number of attempts *trynumber*, the congestion factor σ. Then initialize the initial site of the artificial fish school according to the PSO optimal optimization parameters;

(6) Count the initial fitness of the fish school, and then store the optimal value site and the fitness on the bulletin board;

(7) Artificial fish began to perform the following and the swarming behaviors;

(8) Determine if the site of the artificial fish is advanced. If advance, choose a superior behavior to perform, otherwise perform the preying behavior;

(9) Determine whether the model has reached the maximum number of iterations, if it reaches the maximum number of the iterations, output the optimal artificial fish individual, otherwise go to step 7;

(10) Apply the optimal hyperparameters C, ε and γ to train the prediction model of SVR;

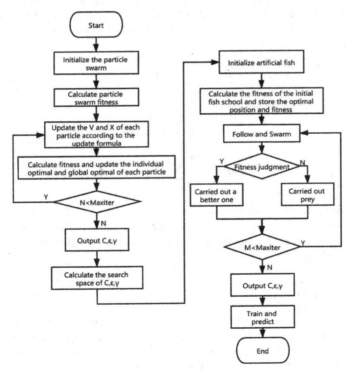

Fig. 1. The flow chart of the PSO-AFSA-SVR algorithm.

(11) Use the water cut prediction model to predict the connection between the time and the water cut of a well.

4 Experiment and Discussion

4.1 Data Description

The experimental data of this experiment are the production data of several oil Wells in an oilfield from 1996 to 2018. And the data of wells numbered 2-2, 2-13, 2-15, 2-19, 2-20, 2-23, 2-34, 2-35, 2-36, 2-46, 2-47 were selected for the experimental data. There are 11 wells in total, and the data of each well includes the production time, the oil layer thickness, the pump diameter, the pump efficiency, the formation coefficient and the water cut. Since all the oil wells are in the same oilfield area, the oil wells in this oilfield are densely distributed and the spacing between the oil wells is small. Therefore, the data distribution of the different oil wells is almost the same. Therefore, data from the multiple oil wells were combined as the experimental data in this experiment.

4.2 Measure Metric

In the experiment of this paper, three evaluation indicators are used to evaluate different models, the Root Mean Square Error (RMSE), Mean Absolute Error (MAE), and Mean Absolute Percentage Error (MAPE), which are defined as follows:

$$RMSE = \sqrt{\frac{1}{n} \sum_{i=1}^{n} (y_i - \hat{y}_i)^2} \tag{1}$$

$$MAE = \frac{1}{n} \sum_{i=1}^{n} |y_i - \hat{y}_i| \tag{2}$$

$$MAPE = \frac{1}{n} \sum_{i=1}^{n} \frac{|y_i - \hat{y}_i|}{y_i} \tag{3}$$

In the above formulas, y_i is the real value of the water cut, $\hat{y}_i$ is the predicted value of the water cut, and n is the total number of the water cut data. Based on the above three evaluation criteria, if a model has the lowest evaluation index value, the model has the best predictive effect.

4.3 Implementation Details

In this paper, the PSO and the AFSA are combined to establish the optimization model. And then compare with other models such as the differential evolution algorithm- SVR (DE-SVR), the genetic algorithm- SVR (GA-SVR), the particle swarm optimization algorithm- SVR (PSO-SVR). Specifically, first take well 2-2 as the test set, and then use the remaining wells 2-13, 2-15, 2-19, 2-20, 2-23, 2-34, 2-35, 2-36, 2-46, 2-47 as the train data set to establish an optimized SVR prediction model. Second, use the optimized SVR prediction model to predict the water cut of well 2-2 over time. Among them, 85% of the train data is used to train the model to obtain three parameters C, ε and γ. After the model is established, the remaining 15% train data is used to validate the model. Finally, the MAPE is used as an indicator to assess the quality of the model.

4.4   Results and Discussion

In the experiment of water content prediction, we compared the predictive value and the real value of DE-SVR, GA-SVR, PSO-SVR and PSO-AFSA-SVR are shown in Fig. 2, Fig. 3, Fig. 4 and Fig. 5, respectively. Among them, the Mc curve in each picture is the true value, and the other curve is the predictive value. It can be seen that although there is a certain difference between the predictive value curve and the real value curve, the overall distinctive between the two is not large, and the change trend of the predicted moisture content curve is basically close to the original curve. Therefore, it indicates that the experiment has obtained a good result. But in the time interval of 60–120, the experimental results are obviously different from the real data, and the fitting effect is not good. Compared with the other three, the SVR prediction model based on hybrid optimization has better experimental performance, for example, the prediction results are closer to the real data in subtle places. In addition, evaluation indicators can be used to more intuitively select the best experimental results. The prediction errors of the four models for well 2-2 are in Table 1. It can be obtained from Table 1 that the PSO-AFSA-SVR model has the lowest prediction error for the moisture content of oil wells in this area, with the MAPE is 0.074300937, the MAE is 4.593158281 and the RMSE is 6.474436672. This proves that the PSO-AFSA-SVR model proposed in this paper has the best experimental results.

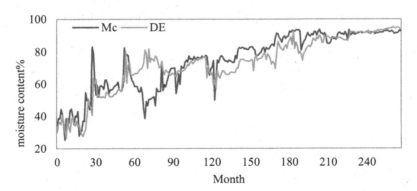

Fig. 2. Comparison of the predicted value of DE-SVR model with the true value.

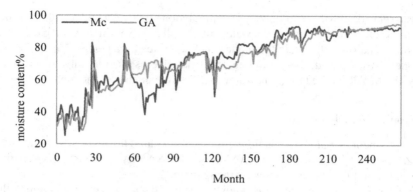

Fig. 3. Comparison of the predicted value of GA-SVR model with the true value.

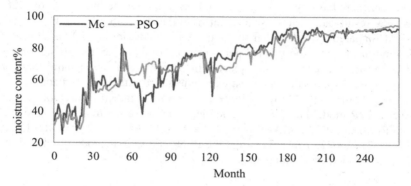

Fig. 4. Comparison of the predicted value of PSO-SVR model with the true value.

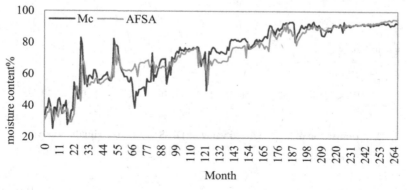

Fig. 5. Comparison of the predicted value of PSO-AFSA-SVR model with the true value.

Table 1. MAPE, MAE and RMSE of four algorithms.

Evaluation index	DE-SVR	GA-SVR	PSO-SVR	PSO-AFSA-SVR
MAPE	0.098442274	0.08096383	0.080530673	0.074300937
MAE	6.189239951	4.975810588	4.949242119	4.593158281
RMSE	9.073529295	7.387674751	7.337648166	6.747436672

5 Conclusions

(1) Aiming at the problem that traditional SVR models are difficult to find the optimal parameters, this paper proposes to use optimization algorithms to optimize the SVR model. After experimental comparison, the model can improve the accuracy of moisture content prediction.

(2) Although there are many optimization methods to optimize the SVR model, the intent of this tractate is to verify that the hybrid optimization algorithm is better than the single optimization algorithm. It can be seen from the experiments in this article that the experimental results of the SVR model based on hybrid optimization have the best prediction results. Which indicates that the selection of the model parameters is very important, and the appropriate parameters will make the model perform better.

(3) The main contribution and achievement of this paper is to propose a new moisture content prediction model based on the hybrid optimized SVR, and it has the higher prediction accuracy.

(4) The change trend of the prediction result based on the hybrid optimization SVR model is not much different from the change trend of the real value, but there is still a big deviation in the details, which indicates that the experimental task still needs improvement. Optimize the hyperparameters of the model is not enough. It is still necessary to find ways to optimize the model from other directions. For example, adding an attention mechanism to the existing model.

Acknowledgement. This paper is supported by the Graduate Innovation and Practice Ability Development Project of Xi'an Shiyou University and its number is YCS21111022.

References

1. Lawal, K.A., Utin, E., Langaas, K.: A didactic analysis of water cut trend during exponential oil-decline. Society of Petroleum Engineers (2007)
2. Yong, L.A., Qi, Z.A., Dw, B., et al.: A fast method of water flooding performance forecast for large-scale thick carbonate reservoirs. J. Petrol. Sci. Eng. **192**, 107227 (2020)
3. Gao, W.J., Yin, R., Yang, J.: Establishment and theoretical basis of the new water-flooding characteristic curve. Acta Petrolei Sinica **41**(3), 342–347 (2020)

4. Bai, T., Tahmasebi, P.: Efficient and data-driven prediction of water breakthrough in subsurface systems using deep long short-term memory machine learning. Comput. Geosci. **25**(1), 285–297 (2021)
5. Holland. J.H.: Adaptation in Natural and Artificial Systems (1975)
6. Eberhart, RC., Kennedy, J.: Particle swarm optimization. In: Proceeding of the IEEE International Conference on Neural Networks, pp. 1942–1948 (1995)
7. Li, X., Shao, Z., Qian, J.: An optimizing method based on autonomous animats: fish-swarm algorithm. Syst. Eng. Theor. Pract. **22**(11), 32–38 (2002)
8. Chen, Y.: Deduction of Wneg's model for watercut prediction. Xinjiang Petrol. Geol. **19**, 403 (1998)
9. Wang, W., Liu, P.C.: The predicting model Gompertz of water-cut rate in water-flood oilfield. J. Xinjiang Petrol. Inst. **13**, 30–32 (2001)
10. Zhang, J.Z., Zhang, L.H., Zhang, H.M., et al.: Usher model for water cut prediction in waterflood field. Xinjiang Petrol. Geol. **25**, 191 (2004)
11. Zhu, T., Li, G., Zhou, W., et al.: Privacy-preserving topic model for tagging recommender systems. Knowl. Inf. Syst. **46**(1), 33–58 (2016)
12. Dou, H., Zhang, H., Shen, S.: Correct understanding and application of waterflooding characteristic curve. Petrol. Explor. Dev. **46**(4), 755–762 (2019)
13. Vapnik, V., Chervonenkis, A.: A note on class of perceptron. Autom. Remote Control **25**, 103–109 (1964)
14. Huang, W., et al.: Railway dangerous goods transportation system risk identification: comparisons among SVM, PSO-SVM, GA-SVM and GS-SVM. Appl. Soft Comput. J. **109**, 107541 (2021)
15. Zhang, L.Y., Zhou, X.F., Fei, T.: Distribution Center Location Problem Solved By ALMM-AFSA algorithm. J. Invest. Med. **63**(8), S65–S65 (2015)

Research on Interlayer Recognition Based on Intelligent Optimization Algorithms and Convolutional Neural Networks

Shaowei Pan[1](✉) [ID], Mingzhu Kang[1], Zhi Guo[2], and Haining Luo[3]

[1] Xi'an Shiyou University, Xi'an Shaanxi 710065, China
[2] Research Institute of Petroleum Exploration and Development, PetroChina, Beijing 100083, China
[3] Research Institute of Exploration and Development, Tarim Oilfield Company, PetroChina, Korla 841000, Xinjiang, China

Abstract. Due to the particularity of interlayer logging curves in reservoirs, as well as the traditional interlayer identification has many problems, such as small amount of data, poor adaptability, low discrimination among interlayer types and strong subjectivity, an interlayer identification method has been proposed based on the intelligent optimization algorithm and Convolutional Neural Networks (CNN) in this paper. In this method, the parameters and structure of the model are optimized by genetic algorithm, particle swarm algorithm and artificial fish swarm algorithm, so that the network model can be adjusted based on the basic architecture and characteristics of the data set. The experimental results show that through the optimization process, three intelligent optimization algorithms are used to build the model structure, and the obtained CNN can avoid artificial selection of the model structure, and evolve a model that is more suitable for the data set, thereby reducing the number of model parameters, shortening the training time and improving the accuracy.

Keywords: CNN · Interlayer · Intelligent optimization algorithm

1 Introduction

Interlayer plays a great role in the dynamic characteristic description of reservoir development. Therefore, in order to realize reservoir dynamic change and accurately predict remaining oil, the distribution law of interlayer must be considered [1]. At present, the methods of interlayer identification are mainly divided into well logging information identification [2], quantitative identification [3], the machine learning method [4].

CNN is a deep feedforward neural network with strong training and optimization capabilities [5]. However, when CNN is used to build the interlayer identification model, with the deepening of network layer, the parameters of the model will increase and the gradient will disappear. Therefore, in this study, the residual network of feature recalculation is designed firstly. The important features of interlayer curves can be improved through feature recalibration convolution. The residual network module can avoid the

S. R. Pokhrel et al. (Eds.): ATIS 2021, CCIS 1554, pp. 13–20, 2022.
https://doi.org/10.1007/978-981-19-1166-8_2

gradient disappearing in the training process and improve the operation speed. At last, due to the waste of computing resources and the complexity of model redundancy in the training process, the genetic algorithm (GA), particle swarm algorithm (PSO) and artificial fish swarm algorithm (AFSA) are proposed to optimize the interlayer recognition model in this paper.

2 Related Works

There are various classification methods for interlayers, mainly from the types and genesis of interlayers [6], lithology and sedimentary causes [7]. The research of interlayers began with core observation and analysis. However, due to limited data from coring wells, high-resolution logging data are usually used by researchers to identify interlayer. For example, Han&liu combined traditional logging curve with inclined logging curve for identification [8].

Some scholars also conducted interlayer identification from both qualitative and quantitative aspects. Such as using logging response characteristics of interlayer insulation to establish interlayer identification standard [9, 10], establishing quantitative identification function [11]. These methods require researchers to have high geological experience, the operation process is difficult to standardize, and the results are uncertain.

In recent years, the rapid development of deep learning technology is very suitable for learning large-scale sample data. For example, Liu et al. [12] applied CNN to well test analysis and proposed a new reservoir identification method. However, there are many CNN structural parameters in the training process, which consumes massive computing resources. In order to avoid the uncertainty of artificial selection of CNN and achieve the optimization effect of the model, the GA, PSO and AFSA are used to optimize CNN.

3 Methodology

3.1 CNN

CNN has been successfully applied to many aspects of computer vision [13]. When deeper networks are able to start converging, with the network depth increasing, accuracy gets saturated and then degrades rapidly [14].

Therefore, JcNet model is proposed, referring to the basic structure of ResNet network, and feature re-calibration convolution modules are added to the network structure of the residual module, as shown in the Fig. 1. Three groups of residual modules are designed to avoid the decrease of model complexity. The input part is 10158 interlayer logging curves, each image size is 224*224. The input module adopts 5*5 convolution kernel with a step size of 2. The global average pool is used instead of the full connection layer, so as to fuse the output of the residual module. The classification layer uses a fully connected layer with 4 neurons and softmax function for image classification. The output is divided into four categories: calcareous, muddy, physical, and reservoir.

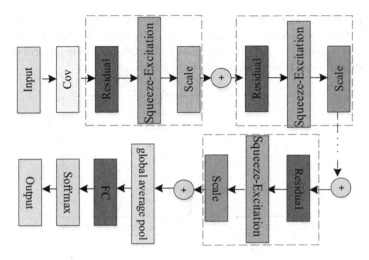

Fig. 1. Experimental model framework

3.2 Intelligent Optimization Algorithm

Intelligent Optimization Algorithm, is developed by simulating or revealing certain natural phenomena or processes. Some common intelligent optimization algorithms include: PSO, GA, AFSA [15].

GA was proposed by Holland [16], which simulates the natural evolution process to search for the optimal solution.

PSO conducts position optimization from population [17], which was proposed by Eberhart and Kennedy. PSO is an algorithm that seeks the optimal solution through the random movement of particle swarm in the initial space.

AFSA was proposed by Li Xiaolei et al. in 2002 [18], which starts to optimize through individual behavior of fish, constantly searching for areas with high food concentration, and gradually approaching the optimal solution.

Therefore, in this paper, three optimization algorithms are used to optimize network hyperparameter and network structure. Iterations, batchsize, learning rate and fixed network structure in JcNet are encoded by GA, PSO and AFSA. The accuracy of the model is selected as the individual fitness function, and the fitness evaluation is performed to evaluate the network, so as to ensure that the network evolves to a more efficient and accurate direction.

4 Experiment and Discussion

4.1 DataSet

The data set used in this study comes from 5 coring wells in a block of Shengtuo Oilfield in China. The type of interlayer of this block is divided into three types: muddy interlayer, calcareous interlayer and physical interlayer. Based on the core data of the coring well, the core depth positioning and logging curve calibration of the five coring Wells were completed in this block. A total of 10158 pictures of logging curves were obtained, and the training set and test set were divided into a ratio of 9:1. The logging curves of three kinds of interlayers and reservoirs are shown in Fig. 2.

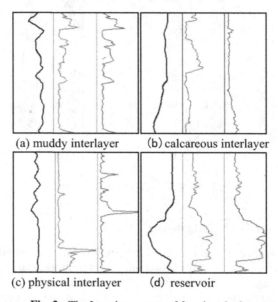

(a) muddy interlayer   (b) calcareous interlayer

(c) physical interlayer   (d) reservoir

Fig. 2. The Logging curves of four interbeds

4.2 Metric Index

Classification Accuracy (Accuracy, A) is used as the evaluation index, which is defined as the ratio between the number of correctly classified samples and the total number of samples for a given test data set. Furthermore, Recall (Recall, R) and F1-Measure (F1) are introduced, and their Macro-averaging (Macro-averaging) is used as the other two evaluation indexes. Macro-averaging refers to calculating the evaluation criteria of this classification, and then calculating the average value of the evaluation criteria of multiple classifications.

The recall rate and its macro average are calculated as follows:

$$R = \frac{TP}{TP + FN} \tag{1}$$

$$Macro\_R = \frac{1}{n} \sum_{i=1}^{n} R_i \tag{2}$$

The F1-measure and its macro average are calculated as follows:

$$F1 = \frac{2TP}{2TP + FP + FN} \tag{3}$$

$$Macro\_F1 = \frac{1}{n} \sum_{i=1}^{n} F_i \qquad (4)$$

In formula (1) and (3), TP means that the positive class is correctly predicted as the number of positive classes, TN means that the negative class is correctly predicted as the number of negative classes, FP means that the negative class is incorrectly predicted as the number of positive classes, and FN means that the positive class is incorrectly predicted as the number of negative classes. In formulas (2) and (4), represents the recall rate or F1-Measure values.

4.3 Implementation Details

The experimental parameters and network structure are coded according to Table 1. Among the three optimization algorithms, the number of population is 10 and the number of iterations is 173. In the three optimization algorithms, the population size is 10, and the number of iterations is 173. The GA mutation probability is 0.001; the maximum number of AFSA predation attempts is 100, the maximum displacement ratio of fish movement was 0.5, the visual field range was 0.3, and the crowding threshold was 0.5.

Table 1. Experimental parameter coding mode

The parameter name	setup
Learning rate	[0.01, 0.001]
Iterations	[10, 100]
Batchsize	[8, 32]
Convolution kernel size	[3, 5, 7]
Convolution kernel number	[16, 128]
Selection of network structure	[Convolution layer, Residual module + feature calibration module, fully-connected layer, global average pooling layer]

4.4 Results and Discussion

The optimization selection process of numerical parameters of the three optimization algorithms is shown in Fig. 3, Fig. 4 and Fig. 5.

The process of learning rate selection of the optimization algorithm during 173 iterations is shown in Fig. 3. After 60 iterations, the learning rate of GA is about 0.006. PSO tends to about 0.01 after 140 iterations. After 92 iterations, the learning rate of AFSA is basically stable between 0.007 and 0.008. The number of batchsize selected by the three optimization algorithms is shown in Fig. 4. The batchsize selection of GA and PSO is 4, and the final selection of AFSA is 11. The fitness changes of the three optimization algorithms in the iterative process is shown in Fig. 5. With the increase of Epoch, the loss of the three optimized JcNet models gradually decreased and became stable.

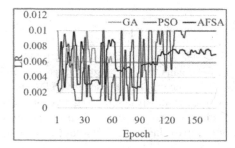

Fig. 3. The curve of learning rate change selected by three optimization algorithms

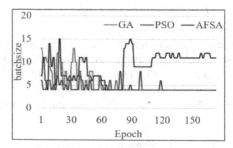

Fig. 4. Batchsize change curve selected by three optimization algorithms

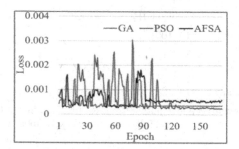

Fig. 5. Fitness change curves of the three optimization algorithms

The information of six CNN models on the test set is shown in Table 2. We can see that the accuracy of deep learning model of JcNet is at least 1.87% higher than that of VGG11 and GoogleNet, and the average recall rate and macro average F1 are about 2% higher, which shows that JcNet has certain advantages in the recognition of interlayer. By comparing the interlayer models established by the three optimized JcNet, we can see that the number of parameters of GA-JcNet, PSO-JcNet and AFSA-JcNet is reduced by 6.83%, 18.67% and 18.85%, respectively, compared with the original JcNet.

According to the experimental results, it can be seen that the accuracy of the three optimization models is improved by 0.09%-0.19%. Especially, AFSA-JcNet took only

409.90s of training time to build the interlayer recognition model, which is 31.10% lower than that of JcNet.

Table 2. Performance and basic information of six CNN models on test sets

Model	Accuracy	Macro average recall rate	Macro average F1	Number of parameters	Model size /M	Training time /s
VGG11	93.20%	0.93	0.93	6583140	50.3	835.13
GoogleNet	93.30%	0.95	0.93	9275628	76.2	1039.49
JcNet	95.17%	0.97	0.95	1604165	12.4	594.96
GA-JcNet	95.26%	0.97	0.95	1494533	11.5	822.64
PSO-JcNet	95.36%	0.97	0.96	1304709	10.1	737.56
AFSA-JcNet	95.26%	0.97	0.95	1301829	10.1	409.90

5 Conclusions

In view of the particularity of interlayer logging curve in reservoir, the interlayer identification model based on intelligent optimization algorithm is proposed, and the applicability of the model is tested on the existing data. This study provides an important contribution to advance the identification of interlayer.

(1) Feature recalculation convolution and residual network is used to establish the JcNet, GA, PSO and AFSA are used to optimize the structure and parameters of the JcNet.
(2) Compared with the original JcNet model, the finally established interlayer recognition model shortens the training time and reduces the model parameters. Moreover, the model shows great accuracy and excellent performance in the interlayer classification.
(3) There are still shortcomings and limitations in this study. In this paper, the choice of random parameters will make the hardware bear great pressure, so the method of transfer learning can be used for pre-training in future research.

Acknowledgement. This paper is supported by the Graduate Innovation and Practice Ability Development Project of Xi'an Shiyou University and its number is YCS21111021.

References

1. Xue, Y., Cheng, L.: The influence of interlayer of bottom water reservoirs during the development stage. Pet. Sci. Technol. **31**(8), 849–855 (2013)

2. Yang, B., Long, Y., Qi, H.: Study on Donghe sandstone intercalation identification based on well longing in Hoilfield. J. Heilongjiang Univ. Sci. Technol. (2015)
3. Hou, Q., Jin, Q., Li, W., et al.: Calcareous interlayer causes and logging identification for the shawan formation of the Chunfeng oilfield. Open Petrol. Eng. J. **10**(1), 134–142 (2017)
4. Liu, J.: Potential for evaluation of interwell connectivity under the effect of intraformational bed in reservoirs utilizing machine learning methods. Geofluids **2020** (2020)
5. Chua, L.O., Roska, T.: The CNN paradigm. IEEE Trans. Circ. Syst. I: Fund. Theory Appl. **40**(3), 147–156 (1993)
6. Liu, X., Cong, L., Ma, S., et al.: Quantitative identification of interlayer in delta phase oilfield. In: IOP Conference Series: Earth and Environmental Science, vol. 781, no. 2. IOP Publishing (2021)
7. Guo, J., Wang, W., Tan, J., Peng, Q., Zhang, D.: Fine characterization method for interlayers in complex meander river sandstone reservoir: a case study of um7 sand of C oilfield in bohai bay area. Int. J. Geosci. **10**(04), 405 (2019)
8. Han, R., Liu, Q., Jiang, T., et al.: Feature, origin and distribution of calcareous interlayers: a case of Carboniferous Donghe sandstone in Hade Oil Field, Tarim Basin, NW China. Petrol. Explor. Dev. **41**, 475–484 (2014)
9. Zhang, Q.G., Zhang, L., Ge, Y., et al.: Identify Interlayer Insulation by Using Logging Data (2016)
10. Zhang, P., Zhang, J., Xu, S., et al.: Genesis, identification and distribution of the interlayer in rhythmic layering in continental low permeability reservoirs. Int. J. Innov. Appl. Stud. **4**(2), 311–316 (2013)
11. Hou, Q., Jin, Q., Li, W., et al.: calcareous interlayer causes and logging identification for the shawan formation of the Chunfeng oilfield. Open Petrol. Eng. J. **10**(1) (2017)
12. Liu, X., Zha, W., Qi, Z., Li, D., Xing, Y., He, L.: Automatic reservoir model identification method based on convolutional neural network. J. Energy Res. Technol **144**, 043002 (2021)
13. Le Cun, Y., Jackel, L.D., Boser, B., et al.: Handwritten digit recognition: applications of neural network chips and automatic learning. IEEE Commun. Mag. **27**(11), 41–46 (1989)
14. He, K., Zhang, X., Ren, S., et al.: Deep residual learning for image recognition. In: Proceedings of the IEEE Conference on Computer Vision and Pattern Recognition, pp. 770–778 (2016)
15. Shen, W., Guo, X., Chao, W., Wu, D.: Forecasting stock indices using radial basis function neural networks optimized by artificial fish swarm algorithm. Knowl.-Based Syst. **24**(3), 378–385 (2011)
16. Holland, J.H.: Adaptation in Natural and Artificial Systems, Ann Arbor (1975)
17. Kennedy, J., Eberhart, R.: Particle swarm optimization. In: ICNN95-International Conference on Neural Networks. IEEE (2002)
18. Chen, K., Li, S.: The study of grid task scheduling based on AFSA algorithm. Int. J. Comput. Appl. Technol. **44**(2), 145 (2012). https://doi.org/10.1504/IJCAT.2012.048685

Near Real-Time Federated Machine Learning Approach Over Chest Computed Tomography for COVID-19 Diagnosis

Yang Cao^(✉) 🆔

School of IT, Deakin University, Geelong, VIC 3216, Australia
caoyang@deakin.edu.au

Abstract. During the COVID-19 pandemic, artificial intelligence (AI) plays a major role to detect and distinguish between several lungs diseases and diagnose COVID-19 cases accurately. This article studies the feasibility of the federated learning (FL) approach for identifying and distinguishing COVID-19 X-ray images. We trained and tested FL components by using the data sets that collect images of three different lungs conditions, COVID-19, common lungs and viral pneumonia. We develop and evaluate FL model horizontally with same parameters and compare the performance with the classic CNN model and the transfer learning approaches. We found that FL can quickly train artificial intelligence models on different devices during a pandemic, avoiding privacy leaks that may be caused by such a high resolution personal and private X-ray data.

Keywords: Machine learning · Federated learning · Privacy security

1 Introduction

Since the first patient was found in Wuhan, Hubei Province, China at the end of 2019, more than 271 million people worldwide have been infected with COVID-19 and more than 5.31 million people have died from it. COVID-19 is an infectious disease caused by severe acute respiratory syndrome coronavirus type 2, and more than 50% of infected patients have abnormal chest X-ray findings [8]. The spreading pandemic has caused the existing healthcare systems in many countries to be on the brink of collapse, including even the Brazilian National Health Service, which is considered to be the most successful healthcare system in Latin America [21]. Medical staff are faced with the unprecedented challenge of identifying COVID-19 cases and the extremely high risk of infection. Machine learning models have the potential to provide safer, more efficiently and more precise results for COVID-19 detection [10].

Machine learning can detect COVID-19 infection based on different medical tests, such as routine blood tests, CT, and chest radiographs [5]. The most

S. R. Pokhrel et al. (Eds.): ATIS 2021, CCIS 1554, pp. 21–36, 2022.
https://doi.org/10.1007/978-981-19-1166-8_3

common method for ML models to identify COVID-19 cases is to detect radiographic images of the patient's chest [3,22]. So far, the existing ML models mainly use convolution neural networks to conduct centralized training on chest X-ray images for COVID-19 recognition because the CNN model is simple and successful in capturing local features [1,27]. And it is not feasible to collect and process data from all hospitals around the globe into a centralized ML server because the data collection process takes a lot of time, but COVID-19 needs to be tested in a short time. Also, patient privacy protection is an important issue that we need to focus on, because the leakage of patient privacy may cause moral issues and increase patient anxiety in social circles [14]. But centralized learning cannot provide effective protection for patient privacy because the deep neural network model stores and trains the data centrally, and can reproduce the training data, which is vulnerable to privacy attacks and cause personal privacy disclosure [20].

Our primary objective in this paper is to train a CNN-based federated learning model to analyze the feasibility of decentralized learning to identify COVID-19 from chest radiographs automatically, which can provide protection for patient privacy by avoiding the exchange of large data sets between server and clients geographically far from each other. In addition, the FL model is compared with the classic centralized learning CNN model and the ResNet model with transfer learning to evaluate the overall performance.

1.1   Motivation

We conduct this research on federated learning approach for detection of COVID-19 computer tomography images to verify the feasibility of using federated learning to detect COVID-19 under the premise of data privacy protection where data is Non-IID.

First, we used the same parameters and data to train models with three different training modes, and compared the training time of centralized, decentralized and transfer learning. Then, we studied the performance differences of three different neural network models with the same parameters. Finally, we discussed the causes of false negatives and the negative impact of Non-IID data on the FL model prediction accuracy.

In medical testing, the medical model requires a high recall rate because it requires to successfully diagnose the diseased person as much as possible. From Fig. 1, FL model and the CNN model have similar recall rates for different lung diseases, and the FL model's recall rate for viral pneumonia is even higher than the CNN model. Therefore, FL has great potential for COVID-19 identification.

1.2   Contributions

The main contributions of this research are outlined as follows:

1. Using a decentralized learning method, the FL model used to identify COVID-19 is trained without infringing on data privacy and obtains an accuracy of 80%.

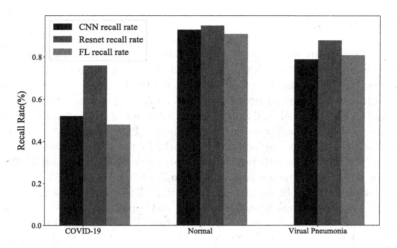

Fig. 1. Three model prediction recall rate

2. FL model perform similar recall rates for different lung diseases to CNN model and get higher recall rate for viral pneumonia than that of CNN model.
3. By building a FL model, a CNN model and ResNet model, compare and evaluate the prediction performance of centralized learning, decentralized learning and transfer learning on the same data.

This study explores the potential of FL to detect COVID-19 by analyzing patient chest X-rays in a decentralized model that protects patient privacy. The FL model has successfully carried out distributed training on multiple clients, different training results based on multi-class, Non-IID data sets (COVID-19, Normal, Viral pneumonia) showed that the detection performance of FL for different lung diseases is quite different, and the detection precision of viral pneumonia is much higher than that of COVID -19. The most important reason for using Non-IID data in this paper is that it is not common in reality to conform to IID data structure. Therefore, using non-IID data with large deviations for training is more in line with the actual situation, the data distribution with different weights makes the experimental results universal. A comparison of the training results of the three models (FL, CNN, ResNet) with same parameters proved that this phenomenon is universal. And explained that the false negatives of COVID-19 may be one of the main reasons for this phenomenon.

The remainder of this paper is structured as follows. Section 2 review the relevant research about COVID-19 classification. Section 3 presents the dataset and methodologies used in this experiment and a brief explanation of FL, CNN and ResNet. Section 4 summarize the experiment setup and steps; Sect. 5 show details of results, compare the performance of different models and discussion. Section 6 is the conclusion of this paper.

2   Related Work

There have been many studies on the detection of COVID-19 based on machine learning. The use of machine learning combined with X-ray images can quickly improve the efficiency and precision of COVID-19 detection, so as to provide timely treatment for infected people and reduce mortality rate.

Khuzani et al., [17] designed a model which has an optimized set of synthetic features using dimensionality reduction methods. The model does not need to segment the chest lesions, and directly extracts features from the CXR image. They used 84 test samples to predict normal, COVID-19, and non COVID-19 pneumonia. The test accuracy is 89%, 96% and 100% respectively.

Ismael et al., [12] combined feature extraction (ResNet and VGG) and classification (SVM with various kernel functions) methods to develop a CNN model with end-to-end training. They selected 95 chest X-ray images for COVID-19 infection predict. ResNet50+SVM achieved the best results with Accuracy, Sensitivity, Specificity, F1 score, AUC of 95.79, 94.00, 97.78, 95.92, 0.9987. Another study [19] combined particle swarm optimization algorithm (PSO) and ant colony algorithm in feature selection to predict COVID-19, Normal, and Pneumonia. The results showed that the SVM+PSO method achieved an accuracy of 99.86% and an F1 score of 99.08.

Khalifa et al., [15] used Generative Adversarial Networks and transfer learning models ResNet50, Shufflenet, Mobilenet to classify COVID-19 and normal on 75 CT images. GAN is used to increase training data, and the transfer learning model is used to classify CT images. Shufflenet achieved the best performance with precision, recall and F1 scores of 85.33%, 85.33%, and 85.33% respectively. In another study, Das et al., [9] used Xception to build a model according to deep transfer learning to detect COVID-19 through X-rays. The proposed model obtains Accuracy, F-measure, Sensitivity, Specificity, Kappa statistics of 0.974068, 0.969697, 0.970921, 0.972973, 0.971924 respectively.

3   Preliminaries and Relevant Machine Learning Concepts

This section explain the datasets and methods used to classify COVID-19. It presents the datasets and classification method CNN, ResNet and FL principle.

Table 1. Dataset information

Cases	Train	Validation	Test	Total
COVID-19	2531	723	362	3616
Normal	7134	2038	1020	10192
Viral pneumonia	942	269	134	1345
Total	10607	3030	1516	15153

3.1   Federated Learning with Aggregation

FL is a new machine learning method proposed by Google in 2016. Compared with traditional centralized learning, FL essentially builds ML models based on distributed data sets and prevent data leakage.

In FL, it has a centralized global server and multiple clients (mobile devices, IoT devices, etc.). Each client has a local data set and local ML model. The global server contains a centralized ML model, also known as the global model. Each distributed client trains a local model based on a local data set, and shares model parameters and weights to the global model. The server obtains these local models and combines them to form a global model, then global model parameters are sent back to all local models [25, 26]. With repeated iterations, the model can be further trained locally.

All local models are built based on the CNN architecture, and 10 CNN models run in parallel in FL as independent clients. Each local CNN model receives parameters from the same global model to initialize the weights, and trains on the local data set in parallel. After the convolution layer, the pooling layer and the fully connected layer are processed, the updated weight parameters of each local CNN model are sent to the global model for FedAvg algorithm. The main reason why the local model uses the CNN architecture is that it can be trained with the same parameters as the centralized training CNN model and directly compare and evaluate the difference in performance.

In this experiment, we also used the federated average algorithm. Each client does one-step gradient descent on its local model with its local data. Then the centre server will do weighted average on the global model. Client K is indexed by k; Local mini batch size is expressed as B; η is fixed learning rate; The gradient of local model can be written as w_t, the global model update gradient $w_{t+1} \leftarrow w_t - \eta \sum_{k=1}^{K} \frac{n_k}{n} w_{t+1}^k$. Algorithm 1 shows FedAvg pseudo-code [18].

In order to protect patient privacy data during model training, we distribute the data to multiple clients to study the feasibility of FL. Each client can be regarded as a hospital in reality. The model no longer needs to share data across clients, and the universality brought by decentralized learning solves the problem of different data sources.

The FL model in this experiment uses the algorithm1 FedAvg mentioned above, assuming that there are K clients for local model training. The central server sends the initial global model w_t to all local clients at the beginning of the t-th round of joint training. Then each local client splits the local data set into batch size B and performs E rounds of training on the received global model, and then sends the updated weight parameter w_{t+1}^k of the local model back to the global model. After receiving the updated parameters from all local clients, the central server averages all the parameters and global model is updated according to the learning rate η. The updated average will be sent to the local client as the new global model parameters and repeat the process until the global model converges.

Algorithm 1. FedAvg

1: **procedure** SERVER EXECUTES
2:     initialize w_0 (random initialization)
3:     **loop** for each round t=1,2,...50 **Do**
4:         **loop** select all client k=1,2,..,10, for each client $k \in K$ ($K = 10$) in parallel **Do**
5:             $w_{t+1}^k \leftarrow$ **CNN-ClientUpdate**(k, w_t) (local weights)
6:         **end loop**
7:         $w_{t+1} \leftarrow \sum_{k=1}^{K} \frac{n_k}{n} w_{t+1}^k$ (global weights)
8:     **end loop**
9: **end procedure**
10: **procedure CNN-ClientUpdate**(k,w)
11:     Get latest model parameter w_t
12:     **loop** for Each selected client k update w for E=1 epoch of Adam with step-size η
13:         Split local data into batches of size B
14:         **loop** for batch $b \in B$ **Do**
15:             $w \leftarrow w - \eta \nabla \ell(w; b)$
16:         **end loop**
17:     **end loop**
18:     return w to server
19: **end procedure**

Reasons for using FL in this experiment:

1. The medical data used in this experiment belongs to patient data privacy in real life. FL does not need to transmit all data to the central server for calculation, which avoids data privacy leakage.
2. Compared with traditional centralized ML model, the central server of decentralized ML model only undertakes the task of collecting gradient updates, and all model training is completed locally, reducing computational consumption.
3. There is no need to provide mass of data to the central model in advance, and constantly add new data to the local model to achieve continuous gradient updates.

3.2   Convolution Neural Network (CNN)

The CNN architecture is chosen for experimental analysis because compared with other architectures, CNN has two major characteristics. 1. It can effectively reduce the dimensionality of the number of neurons and does not affect the result. 2. For medical images, feature loss often leads to misjudgments. The CNN architecture can effectively retain the images features, and the results obtained are more reliable. CNN has an excellent performance in machine learning problems. Especially in processing image data, it is mainly because CNN uses multiple stages for feature extraction, and these stages can learn representations from the data automatically [2,16]. Input the original image into the CNN model, after multiple stages of processing, the image will be converted into a meaningful representation and predict the output.

Convolution layer, a special type of linear operation used for feature extraction, applies a small number of arrays (kernels) to the input. The network uses the image as an input map (input tensor) in the form of a matrix, calculates the product of the input tensor and each element of the kernel at each position of the tensor and sums them to obtain the corresponding output tensor (feature map) [24], as shown in Fig. 2. Each element of kernel (weight) is set to W, each position feature of the input tensor is set to X, each output bias unit is set to B, and the output of the convolution layer is:

$$a = W_0X_0 + W_1X_1 + ... + W_nX_n + B \tag{1}$$

In this experiment, ReLu is used as activation function and set the activation function to R. With the above formula, the first neuron in the second layer can be expressed as:

$$y = R(W_0X_0 + W_1X_1 + ... + W_nX_n + B) \tag{2}$$

The pooling layer is simply a down-sampling operation. The main function is to reduce the dimension of the data to reduce the size of the data, and it can also effectively avoid over-fitting. In this experiment, max-pooling is used to perform data dimension reduction, max-pooling extracts the maximum value in the pooling window and generates a new feature map.

The final main layer of the CNN architecture is the fully connected layer, as shown in Fig. 3. The dense layer accepts all the data processed by the convolution layer and the pooling layer, and the output layer classifies the final result.

Residual Network (ResNet)

ResNet is used as a transfer learning technique in this experiment. Compared with traditional techniques that rely on large data sets to improve performance, transfer learning uses knowledge in different but related fields to improve performance, reducing the dependence on data size [6]. Compared with traditional feature learning, residual learning is relatively easier, because the residual value is relatively small, learning content is less and faster. The residual unit is shown as below:

$$y = x_i + F(x_i, W_i) \tag{3}$$

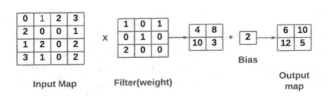

Fig. 2. How classic CNN works?

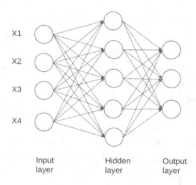

Fig. 3. Fully connected layer

The main technology used by ResNet is the residual network. At the beginning of the design, the residual network mainly served the convolution neural network, and showed excellent performance in image recognition and classification. The residual network solves the degradation problem of the traditional deep CNN network.

In the deep CNN network, set the learned feature to H(x) when the input is X, then the residual can be obtained as F(x)=H(x)-X, learning features can be converted into H(x)=F(x)+X. When F(x) is 0, the accumulation layer is equivalent to only doing identity mapping, H(x)=X. But in fact, the residual cannot be 0, so the layer learn new features according to the input features to obtain better performance. The residual learning structure is shown in Fig. 4 [11].

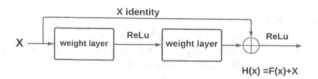

Fig. 4. Residual learning block

4   Setup Details

4.1   Dataset

The experiment was conducted on three sets of chest X-ray data sets. COVID-19, normal and viral pneumonia X-ray images data collection are provided by researchers from Qatar University, Doha, Qatar, and the University of Dhaka [7, 23]. COVID-19 images data collection contains 3616 CXR images from infected cases. Normal lung images data collection contains 10192 CXR images and Viral Pneumonia X-ray images data collection contains 1345 CXR images. The original size of all CXR images from the dataset is 256 * 256 pixels. In this experiment, all X-ray images are resized to 224 * 224 pixels. The data set is divided into training, validation and test sets according to the ratio of 7:2:1. Table 1 presents the number of images in train, validation and test datasets in this study.

4.2 Hardware

All experiments use Python 3.7 and Keras packages, and all code are implemented on the Google Colab Graphical Processing Unit (GPU) Tesla V100-SXM2 which contain 16 GB RAM.

We have developed a deep learning model, a FL model and a ResNet model base on CNN. In addition to the FL model, the other two models will be data exchanged and model training on the central server. Three models are finally tested on the same test data set to verify the feasibility of decentralized training. The local model of FL and the CNN model use exactly the same structure and parameters, and all three models use exactly the same fully connected layer parameters to facilitate comparison.

4.3 Federated Learning Model

In FL model, we distributed the data to 10 clients ($K = 10$) for training. After each client trained 1 Epoch ($E = 1$), the updated model parameters are sent back to the central server for averaging, repeat this process for 50 rounds ($t = 50$). As mentioned above, each local model in FL can be regarded as an independent CNN model. Therefore, the convolution layer, pooling layer and fully connected layer of all local models use the same parameters as the CNN architecture of Table 2. The detailed CNN model setup information is explained in Sect. 4.4, and are not repeat it here.

4.4 CNN Model

A CNN model (same to local model in FL model) is proposed to identify patients as positive for COVID-19, normal lungs and viral pneumonia by analyzing the input chest X-ray images. Each layer in the model processes the input image and converts it into the input image of the subsequent layer for further processing. The X-ray image of the dataset will be adjusted to 224×224 pixel and used as the input size of the CNN model.

After the input layer, create two convolution layers, the kernel size is 3×3, the depth is 32 and use the same size of padding. After that, create a 2×2 maximum pooling layer to reduce the dimensionality.

ReLu is used in all convolution layers as an activation function. The fully connected layer receives the features of all previous layers and puts them together, and uses softmax as the activation function to normalize the output of the fully connected layer.Table 2 summarizes all the parameters, activation functions and structures used in the CNN network.

Table 2. CNN model architecture

	Kernel Size	Activation function	Max-pooling	Dropout
Convolution layers	[3 × 3 × 32] ×1	ReLu	2 × 2	0.2
	[3 × 3 × 64] ×1	ReLu	2 × 2	0.2
Fully connected layers	No. of neurons	Activation function		Dropout
	64	ReLu		–
	3	Softmax		–
Batch size	Learning rate	Optimizer	Epochs	Steps
32	1e−4	Adam	50	20

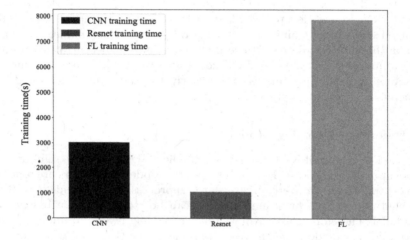

Fig. 5. Training time

4.5   Transfer Learning Model

In this experiment, ResNet was used as a transfer learning model for migration learning to classify lung X-rays because it has been pre-trained on the ImageNet dataset. To a certain extent, the problem of insufficient training data is solved. Since the input of ResNet can only be a three-channel image, but the original X-ray image is a single-channel grayscale image, the input images are resized to a 224 * 224 * 3 RGB images. Thaw the last 65 layers of the convolution layers for fine-tuning.

Table 3. Test performance

	Training time (s)	Training accuracy (%)	Test accuracy (%)	Test loss (%)
CNN model	3024	92.8	81.7	38.50
ResNet model	1053	91.4	89.7	25.47
FL model	7869	90.6	79.6	43.20

5 Results and Discussions

5.1 Performance Analysis

This research aims to analyze the effectiveness of FL for COVID-19 detection by evaluating the performance of the AI model trained on decentralized data and verified on the test set. Through comparison with traditional centralized learning and transfer learning, the feasibility of decentralized learning is specifically evaluated in terms of training time, test accuracy, and loss.

From the perspective of training time, the FL model uses 7869 s to complete the model training, which is much more than that of both CNN model and ResNet model, as shown in Table 3 and Fig. 5. Since the CNN model and the FL local model use the same structure, we can directly compare the training time of the two models. The FL model uses about 2.5 times the training time of the CNN model. Compared with the centralized training of the CNN model on the central server, the FL model requires distributed training on 10 clients in each round, which greatly increases the computational load. This leads to an increase in the training time of the FL model.

The training accuracy and loss of CNN model, ResNet model and FL model with same parameters are visualized in Fig. 6, 7 and 8. During the training process, ResNet model performed better accuracy than CNN and FL. On the way, it was shown that the convergence speed of the ResNet model was much faster than that of the shallow CNN model, and the training and validation accuracy was higher than the CNN model by about 10%. The FL model obtains a loss which is close to the ResNet model, but slightly higher than the CNN model, Table 3 and Fig. 9 show them.

After training the FL and traditional models, predict the result (COVID, normal, viral pneumonia) base on x-ray images. Prediction accuracy and loss are shown in Fig. 10. For prediction accuracy, FL model get a accuracy 79.6% which is close to that of CNN model 81.7%. And the prediction loss 43.2% of the proposed FL is slightly higher than CNN model 38.50%.

The prediction results analysis of each model for three different chest X-ray are shown in Table 4. The CNN model and the FL model show exactly the same

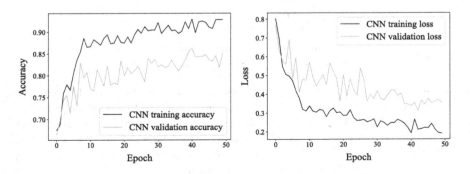

Fig. 6. CNN model training and validation: accuracy and loss

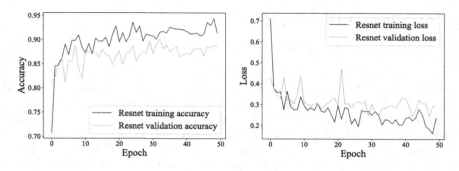

Fig. 7. ResNet model training and validation: accuracy and loss

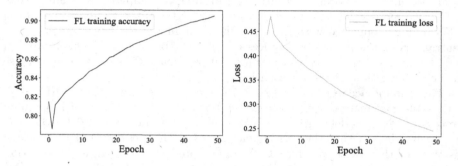

Fig. 8. FL model training: accuracy and loss

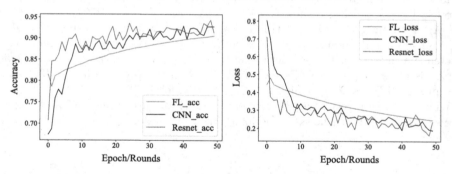

Fig. 9. Three model training: accuracy and loss

accuracy in predicting normal and viral pneumonia, but there are differences in the recognition accuracy of COVID-19. Not only that, the prediction precision of the three models for COVID and viral pneumonia all showed great differences. The predictions precision of the CNN model, ResNet model and the FL model for COVID are 24%,15% and 36% lower than the precision for viral pneumonia respectively. The specific cause of this problem may be the early false negatives of COVID-19 (refer to the discussion section for details).

Therefore, from the perspective of prediction accuracy, it is feasible to use FL to identify and detect COVID-19, because FL and traditional CNN models do not have much difference in prediction accuracy, but federated learning does not require to share data across clients, the central server will not be used for data storage and model training, which is far stronger than the traditional CNN model in terms of privacy protection.

Table 4. Prediction evaluation

		Precision	Recall	f1-score
CNN model	COVID	0.72	0.52	0.6
	Normal	0.83	0.93	0.87
	Viral pneumonia	0.96	0.79	0.87
ResNet model	COVID	0.83	0.76	0.79
	Normal	0.91	0.95	0.93
	Viral pneumonia	0.98	0.88	0.93
FL model	COVID	0.60	0.48	0.53
	Normal	0.83	0.91	0.86
	Viral pneumonia	0.96	0.81	0.88

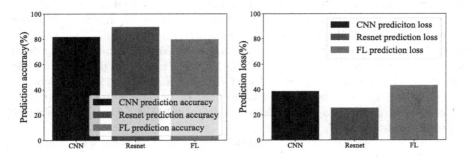

Fig. 10. Three model prediction: accuracy and loss

5.2   Discussion

False Negative
As shown in Table 1, whether in the training or the test set, the number of COVID-19 chest X-ray images is much higher than that of viral pneumonia. However, the recognition precision of the three models for COVID-19 is far lower than the recognition precision of normal lungs and viral pneumonia, as shown in Table 4.

The main reason for this difference is the inherent limitations of computed tomography technology, and false negatives may occur [13]. 50% of patients have normal CT scans within the first two days after the onset of COVID-19 symptoms [4]. The experiment also reflects this problem. Since mass of COVID-19 X-ray images of early COVID were identified as normal lungs, because in the early stage of infection, COVID-19 did not show obvious characteristics on lung X-ray images, which is almost the same as normal lungs. This leads to the inability of the convolution neural network to capture the effective features of COVID-19, which leads to the misjudgement of a large number of COVID-19 images as normal lungs images.

Accuracy Loss

As mentioned above, when using the same parameters, the prediction accuracy of the FL model is slightly lower than that of the traditional CNN model. The reason for the loss of accuracy is that the data set we used in the experiment is Non-IID, that is, non-independent and identically distributed. And the number of the three sets of chest radiographs is quite different, which leads to a high degree of skew in the data. Because the data deviation will cause the weight to diverge, and the FedAvg algorithm updates the global model based on the average weight of the collection, the loss of prediction accuracy is a normal phenomenon.

6   Limitation and Future Direction

This paper uses a Non-IID data set that conforms to the actual situation to verify the feasibility of federal learning to identify COVID-19 automatically through X-ray images under the premise of patient privacy protection. However, this paper did not sort each X-ray image in time series, so there may be differences in the recognition performance of COVID-19 X-ray images in different periods. For example, the X-ray recognition performance of COVID-19 cases detected in the early stage may be far inferior to that of late-stage cases because the X-ray images of early-stage cases have a large number of false negatives which is discussed above.

Discussion section combined with the existing research results to discuss the reasons for the loss of accuracy but did not propose a detailed solution to this problem. The limitation of this paper is that 80% test accuracy is far from sufficient for practical use. Therefore, how to improve the accuracy of the FL model based on Non-IID data is the current challenge. Combined with the findings of this research, two methods may be considered to improve this problem.

1. Formulate structural standards for the training data, and set it as IID data uniformly, so as to avoid the problem of weight deviation caused by Non-IID data.
2. Use pre-training data for weight initialization to reduce the degree of weight deviation

The current research work can only identify known diseases, but unknown epidemic diseases like COVID-19 may still appear in the future. How to quickly detect and identify unknown lung diseases is still a serious problem. This paper proposes an idea here, whether the changes in different parts of the lung X-rays can be compared with the disease symptoms that have been found, such as the texture of the lungs, and an early warning mechanism can be adopted for unknown changes.

7   Conclusion

This study compares the CNN model based on centralized training and the ResNet model with the decentralized FL model based on Non-IID data, and evaluates the feasibility of FL for COVID-19 detection and recognition without infringing the privacy of patients from different aspects. The evaluation results show that the FL model trained on Non-IID data will produce a slight loss of accuracy (2.1%), but this loss is within an acceptable range. FL model perform similar recall rates for different lung diseases to CNN model and get higher recall rate for viral pneumonia than that of CNN model. On the whole, the FL model of decentralized training and the CNN model of centralized training show similar performance, but due to its decentralized characteristics, FL can protect patients' privacy by avoiding data sharing, which is better than traditional centralized training and more suitable for the identification and prediction of medical data.

References

1. Abiyev, R.H., Ma'aitah, M.K.S.: Deep convolutional neural networks for chest diseases detection. J. Healthcare Eng. **2018** (2018)
2. Albawi, S., Mohammed, T.A., Al-Zawi, S.: Understanding of a convolutional neural network. In: 2017 International Conference on Engineering and Technology (ICET), pp. 1–6. IEEE (2017)
3. Arena, P., Basile, A., Bucolo, M., Fortuna, L.: Image processing for medical diagnosis using CNN. Nucl. Instrum. Methods Phys. Res. Sect. A Accel. Spectrom. Detect. Assoc. Equip. **497**(1), 174–178 (2003)
4. Bernheim, A., et al.: Chest CT findings in coronavirus disease-19 (COVID-19): relationship to duration of infection. Radiology **295**, 200463 (2020)
5. Brinati, D., Campagner, A., Ferrari, D., Locatelli, M., Banfi, G., Cabitza, F.: Detection of COVID-19 infection from routine blood exams with machine learning: a feasibility study. J. Med. Syst. **44**(8), 1–12 (2020)
6. Cellina, M., Orsi, M., Toluian, T., Pittino, C.V., Oliva, G.: False negative chest X-rays in patients affected by COVID-19 pneumonia and corresponding chest CT findings. Radiography **26**(3), e189–e194 (2020)
7. Chowdhury, M.E., et al.: Can AI help in screening viral and COVID-19 pneumonia? IEEE Access **8**, 132665–132676 (2020)
8. Cleverley, J., Piper, J., Jones, M.M.: The role of chest radiography in confirming COVID-19 pneumonia. BMJ **370**, m2426 (2020)
9. Das, N.N., Kumar, N., Kaur, M., Kumar, V., Singh, D.: Automated deep transfer learning-based approach for detection of COVID-19 infection in chest x-rays. IRBM (2020)

10. Ghaderzadeh, M., Asadi, F.: Deep learning in the detection and diagnosis of COVID-19 using radiology modalities: a systematic review. J. Healthcare Eng. **2021** (2021)
11. He, K., Zhang, X., Ren, S., Sun, J.: Deep residual learning for image recognition. In: Proceedings of the IEEE Conference on Computer Vision and Pattern Recognition, pp. 770–778 (2016)
12. Ismael, A.M., Şengür, A.: Deep learning approaches for COVID-19 detection based on chest X-ray images. Expert Syst. Appl. **164**, 114054 (2021)
13. Kanne, J.P., Little, B.P., Chung, J.H., Elicker, B.M., Ketai, L.H.: Essentials for radiologists on COVID-19: an update-radiology scientific expert panel. Radiology **296**, E113–E114 (2020)
14. Kayaalp, M.: Patient privacy in the era of big data. Balkan Med. J. **35**(1), 8 (2018)
15. Khalifa, N.E.M., Taha, M.H.N., Hassanien, A.E., Taha, S.H.N.: The detection of COVID-19 in CT medical images: a deep learning approach. In: Hassanien, A.-E., Dey, N., Elghamrawy, S. (eds.) Big Data Analytics and Artificial Intelligence Against COVID-19: Innovation Vision and Approach. SBD, vol. 78, pp. 73–90. Springer, Cham (2020). https://doi.org/10.1007/978-3-030-55258-9_5
16. Khan, A., Sohail, A., Zahoora, U., Qureshi, A.S.: A survey of the recent architectures of deep convolutional neural networks. Artif. Intell. Rev. **53**(8), 5455–5516 (2020). https://doi.org/10.1007/s10462-020-09825-6
17. Khuzani, A.Z., Heidari, M., Shariati, S.A.: COVID-classifier: an automated machine learning model to assist in the diagnosis of COVID-19 infection in chest X-ray images. Sci. Rep. **11**(1), 1–6 (2021)
18. McMahan, B., Moore, E., Ramage, D., Hampson, S., y Arcas, B.A.: Communication-efficient learning of deep networks from decentralized data. In: Artificial Intelligence and Statistics, pp. 1273–1282. PMLR (2017)
19. Narin, A.: Accurate detection of COVID-19 using deep features based on x-ray images and feature selection methods. Comput. Biol. Med. **137**, 104771 (2021)
20. Nasr, M., Shokri, R., Houmansadr, A.: Comprehensive privacy analysis of deep learning: passive and active white-box inference attacks against centralized and federated learning. In: 2019 IEEE Symposium on Security and Privacy (SP), pp. 739–753. IEEE (2019)
21. de Oliveira Andrade, R.: COVID-19 is causing the collapse of Brazil's national health service. BMJ **370**, m3032 (2020)
22. Panwar, H., Gupta, P., Siddiqui, M.K., Morales-Menendez, R., Singh, V.: Application of deep learning for fast detection of COVID-19 in X-rays using nCOVnet. Chaos Solitons Fractals **138**, 109944 (2020)
23. Rahman, T., et al.: Exploring the effect of image enhancement techniques on COVID-19 detection using chest X-ray images. Comput. Biol. Med. **132**, 104319 (2021)
24. Yamashita, R., Nishio, M., Do, R.K.G., Togashi, K.: Convolutional neural networks: an overview and application in radiology. Insights Imaging **9**(4), 611–629 (2018). https://doi.org/10.1007/s13244-018-0639-9
25. Yang, Q., Liu, Y., Chen, T., Tong, Y.: Federated machine learning: concept and applications. ACM Trans. Intell. Syst. Technol. (TIST) **10**(2), 1–19 (2019)
26. Zhang, C., Xie, Y., Bai, H., Yu, B., Li, W., Gao, Y.: A survey on federated learning. Knowl.-Based Syst. **216**, 106775 (2021)
27. Zhang, L., Xiang, F.: Relation classification via BiLSTM-CNN. In: Tan, Y., Shi, Y., Tang, Q. (eds.) DMBD 2018. LNCS, vol. 10943, pp. 373–382. Springer, Cham (2018). https://doi.org/10.1007/978-3-319-93803-5_35

Risk Prediction in Real Estate Investment to Protect Against Asset Bubbles

Balachandra Muniyal, Sumith N.(✉), Sriraksha Nayak, and Namratha Prabhu

Department of Information and Communication Technology,
Manipal Institute of Technology,
Manipal Academy of Higher Education,
Manipal 576104,
Karnataka, India
sumith.n@manipal.edu

Abstract. The real estate market is increasing at a rapid pace, which has also led to increase in risk of investment in real estate. In this paper analysis of real estate markets and prediction of the risk involved in the investment has been done. The approach proposed here clusters the property based on market value per square feet located in different school districts. This also help buyers to make scientifically based decisions on investing in property. The result demonstrate that tat the proposed prediction model estimates approximate value for their property. The prediction give a lower as well as upper limit on the market value of the property. This prediction can safeguard against asset bubbles that are created by various parties involved in real estate network. We can conclude that when buyers and investors are aware of the market price of the asset in future they can safeguard themselves from asset bubbles. Thus, this work is also used to protect against asset bubbles.

Keywords: Market · Linear regression · Clusters · Prediction model · Asset bubble

1 Introduction

Investment is a business activity that interests lot of people in this globalization era. Investments can be done in several ways like buying a house/land or property, which is also termed as real estate. The main participants of real estate market are buyers, sellers and brokers/agents. Property investment has increased at a rapid rate. One of the main reasons for increase in demand of property is the high population rate. According to a statistical data there is lot of young population who have age approximately of 30 years. The result of this data indicates that the younger generation will need a house in the future says [2].

Real estate prices are directly proportional to inflation because as inflation increases housing value also increases. Real estate also have the capacity to generate very high profits due to lack of transparency of individual property and

© Springer Nature Singapore Pte Ltd. 2022
S. R. Pokhrel et al. (Eds.): ATIS 2021, CCIS 1554, pp. 37–52, 2022.
https://doi.org/10.1007/978-981-19-1166-8_4

strength of different real estate markets. Just like every coin has two faces, real estate transactions also have limitations. The transactions of real estate involve huge transaction costs, thus reducing profits. The fact that real estate has low liquidity is also one of the major drawbacks that makes real estate investment a risky venture.

The real estate business heavily depends on few factors including risk associated with it, some of these risk factors cause serious consequences. Like any other business, market analysis plays an important role in real estate investment. However due to inadequate skills and knowledge or due to under estimating the benefit if market analysis, it has remained as an undervalued asset. In reality, the market analysis can be considered as an essential aspect for evaluation of a real estate investment. Therefore, a good research and understanding the market is crucial to good decision-making. However, like any other domain the real estate business also generates a lot of data. This data has to be transformed in a way that is suitable for data mining techniques to predict real estate market values. To ensure worthy investment, it is important to do scientific analysis and determine the potential risks involved in investment. This also would make the decision, scientific and rational, and introduces risk prevention methods to reduce the loss brought about by the risks says [12].

The main aim of this paper is to predict how the market value across future years. This generates a basic idea of property prices among the real estate participants. Market value variation for every year gives market value trend observation. Further, market value trend gives insight to customers whether or not to invest in a particular property, how much money is safe upon investment. The paper is organized as follows. Section 2 covers the important work and insights in real estate market. Section 3 details out the proposed methodology. In Sect. 4 experiment results are discussed. Finally the impact of the work on asset bubbles is discussed in Sect. 5.

2   Literature Review

Jaen et al. [5] uses neural nets to examine the factors that determine the housing prices. Author examined the transactions in real estate and identified the factors that influence their selling price. Also, they further proposed a model that could predict real estate prices. Their work demonstrated that C&RT produced the good results and used the least number of predictors.

Lim et al. [8] demonstrated how artificial neural networks (ANN) with autoregressive integrated moving average (ARIMA) and multiple regression analysis (MRA) can be used to study the similarities and dissimilarities of predictive performance. These techniques were further used to predict house price of particular country. Authors demonstrated that the mean absolute error (MAE), root mean square error (RMSE) and mean absolute percentage error (MAPE) of the ANN model is smaller when compared with the ARIMA model. Also it was seen that ANN has a lower RMSE and a higher Regression value (R-value) compared to MRA model. Thus, ANN model generates high accuracy compared to ARIMA and MRA models.

Many algorithms are developed by Machine learning and from the data it will build models, and uses those data to predict on new data. [9] used classification, regression, neural network and deep learning to predict house price based on various factors which affects house demand and supply. Their work demonstrates that hybrid regressions are better than Ridge, Lasso or Gradient boosting regression. Prediction accuracy is improved using advanced regression algorithms like Random forest. To detect and predict abnormal transactions Sale Price suggested to build a separate algorithm.

Accaini et al. [1] concluded that the Model Tree and Multivariate Adaptive Regression Splines performed well even with small datasets. [12] performed analysis which helped real estate buyers and sellers to approximate the prices of properties, buildings, lands etc. by using the statistical technique called predictive regression. First construct a data warehouse that contains all the information related to real estate. The data obtained from source is cleansed, integrated, selected and transformed in staging area. The tool used to implement was Visual Basic.Net and Oracle data warehousing toolkit. The system can be used to estimate the current prices of property, land, buildings etc. User friendly GUI can also be obtained. This system ensures efficient data mining since the data training is provided by data warehouse MASTERDW. Training data selection criteria are limited to a subset of features in data of data source. No consideration is done regarding any other possible economic trends. Data warehouse does not have any updating technique which may act as an obstacle in obtaining.

Alfiyatin et al. [2] predicts house prices using NJOP houses in the city of Malang using particle swarm optimization(PSO) and regression analysis. PSO is useful for selecting dependent variables. Regression analysis determines the optimal coefficient. Linear regression and particle swarm optimization have been used to predict real estate market. The model used is hedonic pricing, where the value of a property is equal to sum of all its attributes values. The future scope is to obtain the smaller error prediction values.

Wang et al. [11] proposes Support Vector Machine (SVM) and rough sets algorithms to model the pricing on the basis of hedonic price. Rough set is used to reduce numbers of price indicators, which in turn reduces the dimensions of the input space of SVM. The reduced data is used by SVM. This results in improved convergence speed and the forecast accuracy. The method presented here is a combination of both RS theory and SVM. RS has advantage of evaluating large-scale data, removing redundant information and other domains to decrease the training data of SVM, thus eliminating the limitation of SVM algorithm which has low processing speed due to usage of large scale data. Considering RS as a pre-system, then under the information structure pretreated using RS method, a SVM data prediction system is generated.

Li et al. [7] used Support vector machine (SVM) approach for prediction of market. SVM makes use of its some properties which is having benefit of risk minimization principle, using structured the study sample. Structured study sample considered here is very small and non-linear hence analysis of risk factors during investment in real estate projects is done easily. Finally a model based on SVM is developed. This model is very effective and has practical applications as well.

Madhuri et al. [10] developed a real estate web application using tools like Microsoft ASP .NET and SQL 2008. Application provides features for the seller to login to the system and to add new advertisements or remove existing information. Website takes customers specifications and then combines the application of Naive bayes algorithm of data mining. They used classification algorithm to predict house price. Main objective of the paper is to predict the house price for real estate customers based on their budgets and priorities. Future scopes is that more cities can be added which will provide the user to explore more estates and reach an accurate decision.

Bhagat et al. [4] used linear regression algorithm to predict house price. The objective is to predict the house prices to reduce the problems faced by the customer. The method currently used is out dated and involves high risk. So to overcome this problem they developed an updated and automated system. The new system which they developed is cost and time efficient and also contains many simple operations. Every details of each property will be included to provide more details of a required property. The method they used helps the system to run on larger scale.

The literature propose many refinement to main body of work. However, the risk involved in market investment is not demonstrated accurately. In our work, we aim to use this main body of work and add our contribution in analyzing the risk involved by demonstrating the influence of various factors on the real estate price.

3 Methodology

Like any other study involving raw data, the initial steps are carried out to ensure that data is available in required form and format to be suitable for the application. The next steps would be developing the model for the application. These steps are shown in Fig. 1 and can be described as follows: These steps along with the results are explained in the following sections.

3.1 Dataset

Dataset collection: Collected Data set contains data from year 2009 to 2012 of New York City. This dataset consists of 69 features and 580 tuples. 69 features such as market value per sq. ft., tax_year, bbl (Borough, Block and Lot), school District, Zip, $year_built$, $gross_sqft$ and so on. It has numerical data as well as categorical data. In the next step data is preprocessed as required for the application. Missing values and uniformity in the metrics are taken care appropriately.

3.2 Feature Extraction

This step is carried out in two ways. Firstly, to have an initial idea of market value trend subset properties are extracted from dataset which have market value for all four years as seen in Fig. 2 and Fig. 3. Further, to plot the market value

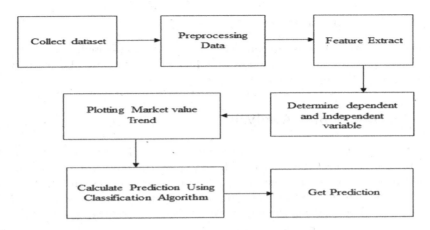

Fig. 1. Design methodology

based on different School Districts within each Borough area features like school district and borough code are selected. This gives an idea of how the features are related to the investment decisions.

3.3 Determine Dependent and Independent Variables

The dependent and Independent variables are plotted in the graph to see their correlation. Our approach uses regression method to find the dependent and independent variables. n statistics, linear regression is a linear approach to modelling the relationship between a scalar response and one or more explanatory variables (also known as dependent and independent variables). Regression approach is a popular method to find the correlation between variables in a dataset. It shows the effect of one feature over the others. Correlation coefficient that lies in the range $[-1, 1]$ is a metric that gives the quantitative value on the impact between two variables. The most popular method to fit a regression line in the XY plot is the method of least-squares. This process determines the best-fitting line for the data. Figure 12 and Fig. 13 shows the influence of the independent variables on the dependent variables

3.4 Market Value Trend

The features extracted are used to study the influence of these features on market investment. Firstly, full market value and market price per sqft for each property with tax year is plotted to have initial idea of market value trend. This is as seen in Fig. 2 and Fig. 3. Further, one can analyze impact of location on market value. The properties are divided based on their borough code. Further, School Districts within each Borough area are analyzed against the market values as seen in Figs. 3, 4, 5, 6, 7 and 8.

3.5   Predict Real Estate Risk

Predictive regression models are suitable for real estate risk prediction. Box plot and density plot are the two models mainly used to compare the predictions with and without comparable 3 attributes.

4   Experiment and Analysis

Real estate involves many aspects that have to be analyzed in order to under-stand its impact on the investment. In this paper we conduct various experiments to confirm that there are few features that actually impact the investment. It is those features that have to be kept in mind when an investment decision has to be taken. The following experiments have a conclusive result to prove this.

4.1   Price Trends and Co-Ops

We start by understanding the full market price as well as market price per sqft of the co-ops. For this purpose, a subset property is chosen which have market value for all four years from year 2009 to 2012. Their market value for studied to have an initial idea of the market value trend as seen in Fig. 2 and Fig. 3. It is seen from this analysis that property rate of property related to certain Borough codes have increased linearly across the years. Also one can see a dip in property rates for few. There is also a sharp spike in property rate for specific real estate items which could be the asset bubble to be discussed later.

4.2   School District and Borough Codes

In this work, to check the influence of location on the market value, the properties are divided based on their borough code. In school district1, school district2 and school district3, market value increased throughout the four years. It is also our finding that in school district2 not only market value has increased but also market value per square feet is increased compared to the other properties. This is evident in Figs. 4, 5, 6, 7 and 8.

Further, the study revealed important aspects of considering Borough codes for real estate investment. Interesting fact from 4 to 8 is that, for Borough Code 2 market value per sqft decreased from 2009–2011 and increased in year 2012 as seen in 9. This was confirmed further by checking first comparable properties market value per sqft and second comparable properties market value per sqft. The results show that market value per sqft have similar trend as seen in Fig. 10 and 11.

Figure 10 and Fig. 11 shows that Comparable rental 1 market value per sqft and Comparable rental 2 market value per sqft lacks the trend of the co-ops

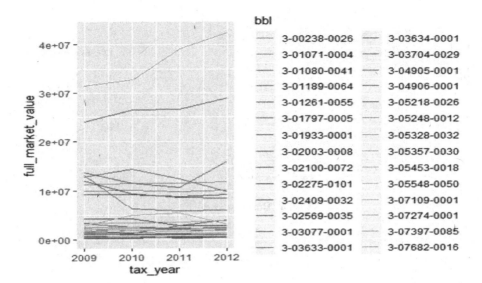

Fig. 2. Full market value per sqft

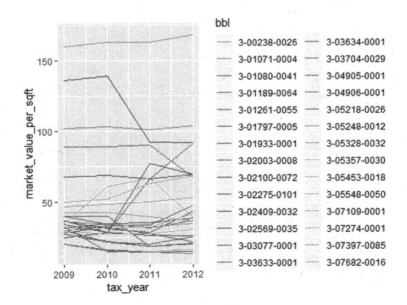

Fig. 3. Market value per sqft

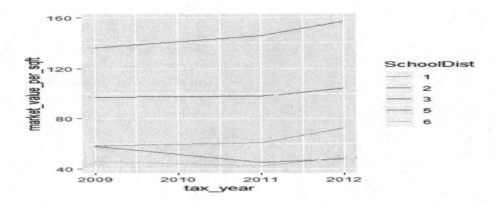

Fig. 4. Borough code 1

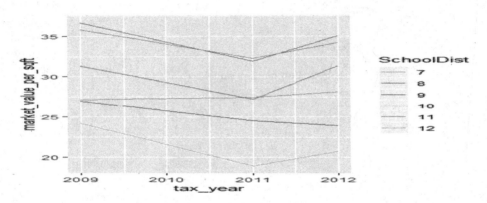

Fig. 5. Borough code 2

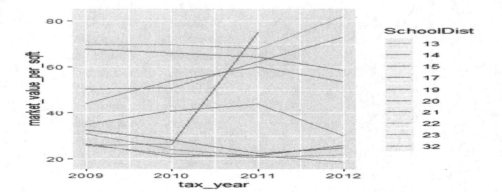

Fig. 6. Borough code 3

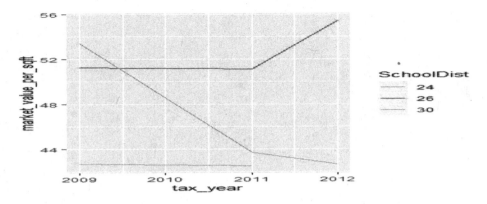

Fig. 7. Borough code 4

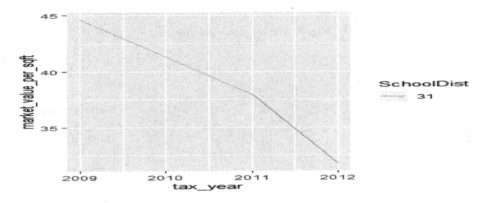

Fig. 8. Borough code 5

4.3   Market Value Estimation

To check whether market value estimation will change by including comparable 3, two models are built using market value per sqft from Year 2012 as response variable and gross income per sqft and expense per sqft from Year 2012 as predictors. First model included only comparable 1 and comparable 2 and second model included comparable 1, comparable 2 and comparable 3. Data set is divided into two set, 2/3 of the dataset will be training data set and 1/3 of dataset will be test data set. Figure 13 and Fig. 14 shows the predicted results from the two model. Plot shows that there is no difference between two predictions that means Comparable 3 does not cause any major change of market value.

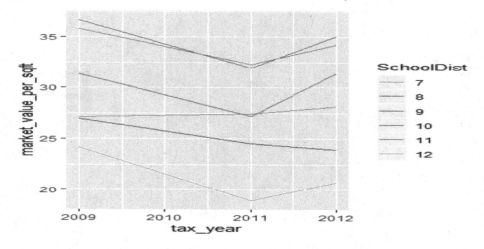

Fig. 9. Market value per sqft

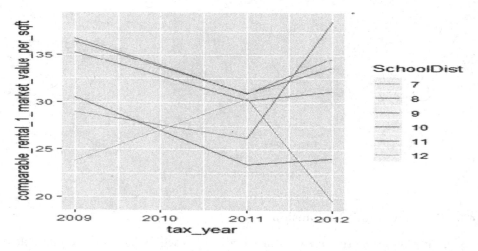

Fig. 10. Comparable rental 1 market value per sqft

5   Cluster the Properties on Its Market Value

K-means is one of the simplest unsupervised learning algorithms that solves the well-known clustering problem. The main idea of k-means is to define k centroids, one for each cluster. These centroids should be placed randomly. The better choice is to place them far away from each other. In the next step, place each point to the nearest centroid. When no point is pending, the first step is completed and an early cluster is done. We can thent re-calculate 'k' new centroids as barycenter's of the clusters resulting from the previous step. After obtaining these 'k' new centroids, data points have to be once again placed to

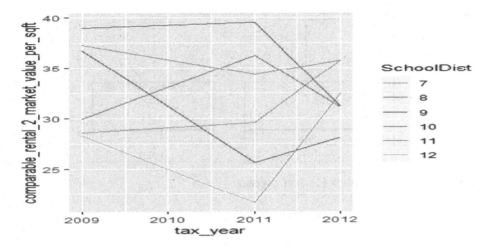

Fig. 11. Comparable rental 2 market value per sqft

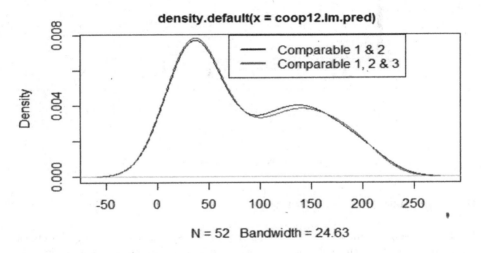

Fig. 12. Density plot

nearest new centroid. After successive iterations clusters are formed.

Figure 15 shows the results of the K-means algorithm applied on the dataset. In this study K-Means has been applied to cluster the properties based on the market value per square feet in different school districts. Three different clusters can be observed in the plot represented by green, black and red colors

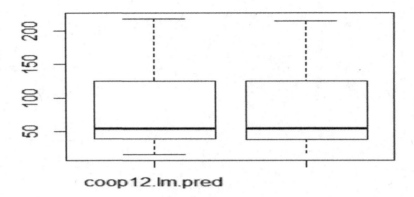

Fig. 13. Box plot

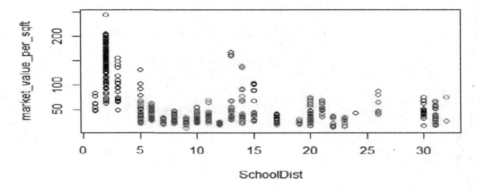

Fig. 14. K-means clustering

6 Expense as a Predictor

In the dataset, estimated expense was not included until Year 2012. To check whether it impacts the selection of comparable properties data set is divided into two sets, 2/3 of the dataset will be as training set and 1/3 as test set. Based on initial analysis two predictive models are built, using market value per sqft as response variable and gross income per sqft, expense per sqft as predictors. Figure 16 includes expense per sqft, while the Fig. 17 does not include expense per sqft.

Mean Square Error is used to evaluate two models. Mean square error is the mean of squares of distance between two market values and is given in Eq. 1.

$$MSE = \Sigma_{i=1}^{k} p_i (x_i - t)^2 \qquad (1)$$

Mean square error for model without expense as predictor is 676.577 and model with expense as a predictor is 274.5491. It shows that model with expense as

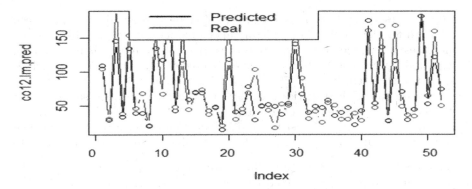

Fig. 15. Model with expense as a predictor (Color figure online)

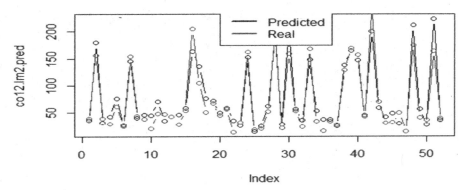

Fig. 16. Model without expense as a predictor

a predictor has more accurate prediction further asserting that expense has an impact on selection of comparable properties.

7 Market Value Prediction

To predict market value divided data set into two sets, 25% of total as test dataset and 75% of total as training dataset. Predicted market value per sqft for different properties are based on their borough code. Predictive Regression is applied on Training Data set. Result of this prediction is on following metrics:

- Residual standard error: It is a measure used to assess how well a linear regression model fits the data. Te experimental results shows that it is 0.3655 on 428 degrees of freedom.
- Multiple R-squared: It represents the proportion of the variance in the response variable that can be explained by the predictor variables of a regression model. It is 0.7415 in our case.

- Adjusted R-squared: It is a revised version of R-squared that has been adjusted for the number of predictors in the model. The adjusted R-squared increases when the new term improves the model more than would be expected by chance. It decreases when a predictor improves the model by less than expected. It is 0.7379.
- F statistic values: F-statistics are based on the ratio of mean squares. It is 204.6 on 6 and 428 degrees of freedom
- P value: The F statistic must be used in combination with the p value when you are deciding if your overall results are significant. It is less than 2.2e−16

The predicted result of market value is stored in csv file with borough code, original market value and predicted market value as shown in the Fig. 17.

	A Boro Code	B Orginal Market Val	C Predicted Market Value	D	E
2	2	32.71	38		
3	1	103	72		
4	3	89	49		
5	3	47.48	41		
6	1	62	39		
7	1	189	177		
8	3	39.31	26		
9	1	196	191		
10	2	26.13	33		
11	1	148	198		
12	3	32.9	30		
13	3	33.4	40		
14	3	25.1	32		
15	2	21.5	33		
16	2	18.57	30		
17	3	75	42		
18	1	95	83		
19	1	93	42		
20	4	67	42		
21	2	29.5	35		
22	4	42.3	29		
23	3	34.5	27		

Fig. 17. Predicted market value

8   Asset Bubbles in Real Estate Investment

An asset bubble in pricing can be considered as asymmetric deviation of the market price of an asset from its real value. It is to be noted that all market participants have access to same information thus resulting in almost similar real price of an asset. Thus asset bubble theoretical has no existence, yet is a possibility in many cases. Existence of irrational participants in the market place and their influence on prices would cause an assset bubble in market. This leads us into the discussion of rational bubbles says [3].

It is often the case that bad economic and investment decisions are due to asset bubbles. Some asset prices are seen during rising phase of the economic cycle. This leads to excessive lending, which further results in the rise of asset prices. This further leads to c lead to excessive risk-taking, especially credit risk. One can observe that there is always a correlation between the cyclical behaviour of the economy and risk perception [6]. This means that although perceived risk declines, the actual risk that might be seen in the future rises during boom times and financial imbalances increase at the same time.

The work carried out in this paper clearly shows the market value of the real estate for subsequent years. With this it is likely to notice that any other market value stating exponentially above this base price would be an asset bubble. This work can be used to identify such bubbles with clarity since the predicted values are already available. A careful observation of the results seen in Fig. 17, shows that the predicted value is much lesser than the actual market rate. This is because the actual rate is a asset bubble caused by real estate participants. As an investor, one can plan and clarify the existence of such bubble before making any investment.

9   Conclusion

In this paper, the data of the real estate market is analyzed using machine learning techniques. Independent and dependent variables are identified to plot the market value trends. In this work, we demonstrated the use of prediction model to predict the price in the real estate market. The results shows the correlation between price and few prominent factors such as sq. feet area and location. The results also gives us a clear picture on price trends across four years. Using the prediction model proposed here one can estimate the rental income. The results also provides clusters among the real estate elements.

Further the paper also discusses how the existence of the asset bubble can be identified by the proposed work. This work helps investors to take a scientifically guided decision in real estate market.

References

1. Acciani, C., Fucilli, V., Sardaro, R.: Data mining in real estate appraisal: a model tree and multivariate adaptive regression spline approach. Aestimum, pp. 27–45 (2011)
2. Alfiyatin, A.N., Febrita, R.E., Taufiq, H., Mahmudy, W.F.: Modeling house price prediction using regression analysis and particle swarm optimization. Int. J. Adv. Comput. Sci. Appl. **8**, 323–326 (2017)
3. Atkinson, P.: Asset price bubble identification and response (2012)
4. Bhagat, N., Mohokar, A., Mane, S.: House price forecasting using data mining. Int. J. Comput. Appl. **152**(2), 23–26 (2016)
5. Jaen, R.D.: Data mining: an empirical application in real estate valuation. In: FLAIRS Conference, pp. 314–317 (2002)
6. Kubicová, I., Komarek, L.: The classification and identification of asset price bubbles (2011)
7. Li, W., Zhao, Y., Meng, W., Xu, S.: Study on the risk prediction of real estate investment whole process based on support vector machine. In: 2009 Second International Workshop on Knowledge Discovery and Data Mining, pp. 167–170. IEEE (2009)

8. Lim, W.T., Wang, L., Wang, Y., Chang, Q.: Housing price prediction using neural networks. In: 2016 12th International Conference on Natural Computation, Fuzzy Systems and Knowledge Discovery (ICNC-FSKD), pp. 518–522. IEEE (2016)
9. Lu, S., Li, Z., Qin, Z., Yang, X., Goh, R.S.M.: A hybrid regression technique for house prices prediction. In: 2017 IEEE International Conference on Industrial Engineering and Engineering Management (IEEM), pp. 319–323. IEEE (2017)
10. Madhuri, C.R., Anuradha, G., Pujitha, M.V.: House price prediction using regression techniques: a comparative study. In: 2019 International Conference on Smart Structures and Systems (ICSSS), pp. 1–5. IEEE (2019)
11. Wang, T., Li, Y.Q., Zhao, S.F.: Application of SVM based on rough set in real estate prices prediction. In: 2008 4th International Conference on Wireless Communications, Networking and Mobile Computing, pp. 1–4. IEEE (2008)
12. Wedyawati, W., Lu, M.: Mining real estate listings using oracle data warehousing and predictive regression. In: Proceedings of the 2004 IEEE International Conference on Information Reuse and Integration 2004. IRI 2004, pp. 296–301. IEEE (2004)

Cognitive Artificial Intelligence Computing Modeling Process in Meta Cognitive Architecture Carina

Ojaswi Bhimineni⑩, Geda Sai Venkata Abhijith⑩, and Srikanth Prabhu$^{(\boxtimes)}$⑩

Department of Computer Science and Engineering, Manipal Institute of Technology, Manipal, Karnataka, India
srikanth.prabhu@manipal.edu

Abstract. In this paper, Cognitive Artificial Intelligence computing modeling process in Meta cognitive architecture CARINA is implemented. Basically in cognitive sciences, cognitive modeling has become fundamental tool to process. Based on the usage of cognitive architectures, cognitive modeling is designed. For the artificial intelligent agents, CARNIA is most widely used and this is a Meta cognitive architecture which is derived from the Meta cognitive Meta model. This Meta cognitive Meta model is based on the Meta cognitive mechanism which will monitor and control the Meta level. Initially, the cognitive task is selected. Next, the information is described for the cognitive task. By using natural language, the cognitive task is described. GOMS also describes the cognitive task. For the obtained data, decision functions and cognitive functions are described. By using artificial intelligence, the data is computed. Now, the data is transferred from Cognitive Model form GOMS to M + + Language. Now, the data will be performed by using cognitive model in CARNIA. At last testing and maintenance will be done very effectively. From results it can observe that accuracy, cost, errors and observation time gives effective result.

Keywords: Meta cognitive architecture · CARNIA · Artificial Intelligence · GOMS (Goals · Operators · Methods and Selection)

1 Intro

The radio spectrum is the unique natural resource totally assigned to different licensed holders according to the fixed spectrum assignment policy. It was then analyzed that a large portion of spectrum is not utilized under time and place [1]. Cognitive radio (CR) was introduced to solve this problem by opportunistically utilizing the spectrum during the absence of their owners. It was considered to play a major role for the utilization of spectrum resources to meet the continuous greatest demand of wireless systems.

Cognitive radio networks (CRNs) enable cognitive users (or secondary users) to sense the environment in order to identify spectrum holes, analyze the parameters, and make decisions for dynamic resource allocation management [2]. These capabilities are realized through integrating artificial intelligence (AI) techniques in the section of the

S. R. Pokhrel et al. (Eds.): ATIS 2021, CCIS 1554, pp. 53–61, 2022.
https://doi.org/10.1007/978-981-19-1166-8_5

CR. AI enables cognitive users to solve problems by emulating human biological processes such as learning, reasoning, decision making, self-adaptation, self-organization, and self-stability.

Various surveys have been introduced in the literature for the applications of AI techniques in CRNs. Basically, the combination of frequency spectrum bands is nothing, but a cognitive radio and it is taken from the innovative radio communication technology. This is distributed using software algorithms. The reserved spectral range will use the cognitive radio for the process. By using primary and secondary users the cognitive radio network will be emerged and this network will divide the data based on the concept used. Fixed frequency ranges are used by the primary users and variable frequency ranges are used by the secondary users. The following functions will show the ability and functions of cognitive radio.

1. Busy Spectrum Bands and
2. Detecting of free sensing

Different types of technologies are used for the detection by the cognitive radio; they are cyclic static detection, coherent filtration, detection by correlation function and power detection. Different learning algorithms are implemented by the cognitive radio.

CR was firstly defined by Joseph Mitola as "a radio that is aware of its surroundings and adapts intelligently". It has been introduced to respond to the under-utilization of spectral resources by dynamically access the temporarily unused spectrum bands. CRNs bring new cognitive radio users (CRUs) that should sense the licensed bands to identify the spectrum holes, and then exploit them as long as they don't interfere with the licensed users [3]. To meet these capabilities, CRN executes the four main functions of the cognitive cycle. These functions are spectrum sensing, spectrum management, spectrum sharing, and spectrum mobility. The below Fig. 1 shows the cognitive radio cycle. In this cognitive radio cycle mainly radio environment, spectrum sensing, spectrum mobility, spectrum management are used.

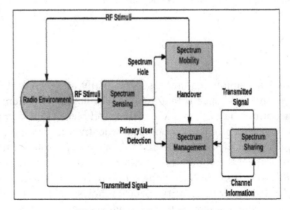

Fig. 1. Cognitive radio cycle

Spectrum sensing is an important function in CRNs using dynamic access. The CRU (Cognitive Radio Unit) must identify available bands for its transmission and be able to detect the presence of the primary users (PUs) [4] to avoid harmful interferences. Spectrum sensing can be done by one or multiple CRUs exchanging information in cooperative way or in competitive manner. Generally, exist three spectrum sensing strategies includes transmitter-based sensing method, interference temperature-based sensing method or through the received Signal-to-Noise Ratio (SNR).

Spectrum management decides and allocates the best available spectrum band among available bands to meet the user transmission requirements and improve his throughput. Spectrum sharing coordinates access among SUs (Sensing Units) and share available spectrum bands between them in fair manner [5]. Spectrum sharing techniques can be classified as inter leaver, underlay, and overlay.

2 Literature Survey

2.1 Survey of Artificial Intelligence Approaches in Cognitive Radio Networks [6]

To improve the capability of the cognitive radio, in this paper by using cognitive radio networks, artificial intelligence approaches are implemented. By evaluating the problems of human biological process, AI will enable the data. Based on the reasoning, decision making, self-organization, self-stability and learning the problems will be solved. By using the spectrum mobility, spectrum sensing, decision making and spectrum sharing, the cognitive radio problems will be solved. Hence in this survey paper is given related to the techniques of cognitive radio which is related to the artificial intelligence.

2.2 Application of Artificial Intelligence in Cognitive Radio for Planning Distribution of Frequency Channels [7]

To increase the efficiency of channels, cognitive radio technology is implemented. While transmitting the frequency channels, the cognitive radio technology is allocated. While transmitting the channels, free channels and busy channels will be there. All these channels will be based on the properties, of channel and these properties will depend on the clusters.

Two-dimensional distribution of frequency channels are designed by using the initial data. This will characterize the data based on the channel distribution. Finite sets are utilized for the frequency channels which are fixed. Here frequency channels might be fixed but the bandwidth will remain same.

The clustering of free and busy channels is investigated in the assumption of random distribution of free and occupied channels for each user. It has been shown that numbers of free and used channels approximately coincide and their sum is 1/3 of the total number of channels, so the number of uncertain channels was 2/3.

2.3 Knowledge-Growing System: The Origin of the Cognitive Artificial Intelligence [8]

It is likewise shown that applying of AI for recurrence assets dependent on this model can lessen the hour of channel search by 10%. The produced factual model of bunching channels is applied to the calculation of AI, specifically support vector machine (SVM). This calculation is applied to channels that communicate VoIP traffic.

Cognitive Artificial Intelligence Method for Measuring Transformer Performance [9]

In this paper, we compute transformer end-of-life assessment utilizing and data combination calculation. This will utilize two boundaries, transformer condition and slope of condition, which are determined by utilizing the condition-Based Sampling Period strategy. Condition created haphazardly, while the inclination of condition is determined by utilizing two conditions from current perception and past perception. This condition is utilized to decide the testing time of the estimation information gathered from sensors. The testing period will be diminished if the state of the transformer weakens. The digression of the condition will be utilized to appraise transformer end-of-data.

Contemporary Cybernetics and Its Facets of Cognitive Informatics and Computational Intelligence [10]

This paper investigates the engineering, hypothetical establishments, and ideal models of contemporary computer science according to viewpoints of Cognitive intelligence (CI) and computational insight. The cutting-edge space and the various leveled conduct model of artificial intelligence are expounded at the goal, autonomic, and intellectual layers. The CI aspect of robotics is introduced, which clarifies how the mind might be mirrored in artificial intelligence through CI and neural informatics. The computational knowledge aspect is depicted with a conventional insight model of robotics. The similarity among normal and computerized knowledge is broke down. A cognizant structure of contemporary robotics is introduced toward the improvement of transdisciplinary hypotheses and applications in computer science, CI, and computational knowledge.

3 Meta Cognitive Architecture Carina

The below Fig. 2 shows the flow chart of Meta cognitive architecture CARNIA. Initially, the cognitive task is selected. Next, the information is described for the cognitive task. By using natural language, the cognitive task is described. GOMS also describes the cognitive task. For the obtained data, decision functions and cognitive functions are described. By using artificial intelligence, the data is computed. Now, the data is transferred from Cognitive Model form GOMS to M++ Language. Now, the data will be run by using cognitive model in CARNIA. At last testing and maintenance will be done very effectively.

3.1 Selection of Cognitive Task

Cognitive agent will use the sentences while syntactic analysis is modeled by the cognitive task.

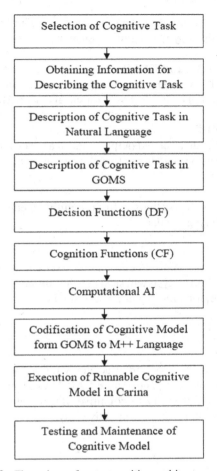

Fig. 2. Flow chart of meta cognitive architecture carnia

3.2   Obtaining Information for Describing the Cognitive Task

By using three experts, the information will be described by the cognitive task. Documentary sources will be conducted by the experts after describing the tasks.

3.3   Description of Cognitive Task in Natural Language

A cognitive agent will analyze the cognitive task in the real world. Generally, cognitive agent will receive a stimulus from environment. Pre-processing stage will perform the data by transferring input stimulus to sensory memory. The problems that occurred during process will be solved by the cognitive agent attention system.

Description of Cognitive Task in GOMS
Cognitive task in GOMS will describe the goals, orders, methods and structures. Cognitive task will perform the GOMS based on the agent's performance.

Decision Functions (DF)
Where the input is taken as data set and output is taken as decision, and then it is known as decision function. Decision function is to estimate the problems in cognitive data.

Cognitive Function (CFs)
Cognitive functions (CFs) will take the data from cognitive agents and solve the problems by determining and analyzing the data.

Computational AI
The main intent of computational artificial intelligence is to refer the specific data by performing specific task. Similarly, it will save the data automatically using small space. Because of this the usage of memory will be very small.

4 Results

The below Fig. 3 shows the comparison of accuracy for cognitive AI architecture and cognitive AI using Meta cognitive architecture CARINA. Compared with cognitive AI architecture and cognitive AI using Meta, cognitive AI using Meta cognitive architecture CARINA improves the accuracy in very effective way.

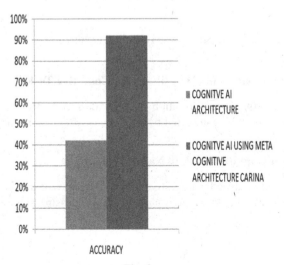

Fig. 3

The below Fig. 4 shows the comparison of cost for cognitive AI architecture and cognitive AI using Meta cognitive architecture CARINA. Compared with cognitive AI architecture and cognitive AI using Meta, cognitive AI using Meta cognitive architecture CARINA reduces the cost in very effective way.

The below Fig. 5 shows the comparison of errors for cognitive AI architecture and cognitive AI using Meta cognitive architecture CARINA. Compared with cognitive AI architecture and cognitive AI using Meta, cognitive AI using Meta cognitive architecture CARINA reduces the errors in very effective way (Table 1).

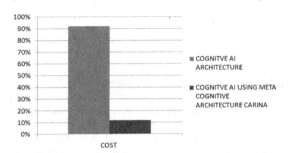

Fig. 4. Comparison of cost

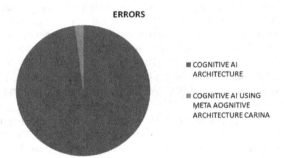

Fig. 5. Comparison of errors

Table 1. Comaprison of cognitive ai architecture and cognitive ai using meta cognitive architecture carina

S.No	Parameter	Cognitive AI architecture	Cognitive AI using meta cognitive architecture CARINA
1	Accuracy	Low	High
2	Cost	High	Low
3	Errors	High	Low

5 Conclusion

In this paper, Cognitive Artificial Intelligence computing modeling process in Meta cognitive architecture CARINA is implemented. Data is transferred from Cognitive Model form GOMS to M++ Language. Now, the data will be run by using cognitive model in CARNIA. Based on the usage of cognitive architectures, cognitive modeling is designed. For the artificial intelligent agents, CARNIA is most widely used, and this is a Meta cognitive architecture which is derived from the Meta cognitive Meta model. From results it can observe that accuracy, cost, errors and observation time give effective results.

References

1. Sumari, A.D.W., Sereati, C.O., Ahmad, A.S., Adiono, T.: Constructing an architecture for cognitive processor based on knowledge-growing system algorithm. In: The Proceedings of 2020 International Symposium on Nano Science and Technology, 30–31 October 2015, pp. 0-04 (2015)
2. Bachri, K.O., Anggoro, B., Sumari, A.D.W., Ahmad, A.S.: Cognitive artificial intelligence method for interpreting transformer condition based on maintenance data. Adv. Sci. Technol. Eng. Syst. J. 2(1), 1137–1146 (2019)
3. Ahmad, A.S., Sumari, A.D.W.: A novel perspective on artificial intelligence: information-inferencing fusion for knowledge growing. In: The 2nd International Conference on Electrical Engineering and Informatics 2019, Keynote Speech Paper, 6 August 2009 (2019)
4. Bednarczyk, W., Gajewski, P.: Hidden Markov models based channel status prediction for cognitive radio networks. In: Proceedings of Progress in Electromagnetics Research Symposium, Prague, Czech Republic, pp. 2770–2773 (2019)
5. Lu, X., Wang, P., Niyato, D., Hossain, E.: Dynamic spectrum access in cognitive radio networks with RF energy harvesting. IEEE Wirel. Commun. 21(3), 102–110 (2019). https://doi.org/10.1109/mwc.2014.6845054
6. Morabit, Y.E.L., Mrabti, F., Abarkan, E.H.: Survey of artificial intelligence approaches in cognitive radio networks. J. Inf. Commun. Converg. Eng. 17(1), 21–40 (2019)
7. Politanskyi, R., Klymash, M.: Application of artificial intelligence in cognitive radio for planning distribution of frequency channels. IEEE (20190). 978-1-7281-2399-8/19/$31.00
8. Datumaya, A., Sumari, W., Ahmad, A.S.: Knowledge-growing system: the origin of the cognitive artificial intelligence. IEEE (2047). 978-1-5386-0475-5/17/$31.00
9. Ahmad, A.S., Bachri, K.O.: Cognitive artificial intelligence method for measuring transformer performance. IEEE (2016). . 978-1-5090-4171-8/16/$31.00
10. Wang, Y., Kinsner, W., Zhang, D.: Contemporary cybernetics and its facets of cognitive informatics and computational intelligence. IEEE Trans. Syst. Man Cybern. Part B Cybern. 39(4), 823–833 (2009)
11. Sklivanitis, G., et al.: Airborne cognitive networking: design, development, and deployment. IEEE Access 6, 47217–47239 (2008). https://doi.org/10.1109/access.2018.2857843
12. Xu, C., Li, Y., Yang, Y., Xian, Y.: A novel spectrum prediction algorithm for cognitive radio system based on chaotic neural network. J. Comput. Inf. Syst. 9(1), 313–320 (2007)
13. Hemmert, F., Becker, P., Görts, A., Hrlic, D., Netzer, D.V., Weld, C.J.: Aicracy: everyday objects from a future society governed by an artifical intelligence. Mensch & Computer (2007)

14. Begel, A.: Best practices for engineering AI infused applications: lessons learned from microsoft teams. In: 2007 IEEE/ACM Joint 7th International Workshop on Conducting Empirical Studies in Industry (CESI) and 6th International Workshop on Software Engineering Research and Industrial Practice (SER&IP) (2007)
15. Kose, U., Vasant, P.: Fading intelligence theory: a theory on keeping artificial intelligence safety for the future. In: 2005 International Artificial Intelligence and Data Processing Symposium (2017). https://doi.org/10.1109/IDAP.2027.8090235

Effectiveness of the Use of Golden Ratio in Identifying Similar Faces Using Ensemble Learning

Gangothri Sanil[1] , Krishna Prakash[1,2](✉) , Srikanth Prabhu[2,3] ,
and Vinod C. Nayak[3]

[1] Information and Communication Technology, Manipal Institute of Technology
(MIT), Manipal Academy of Higher Education (MAHE), Manipal, India
[2] Computer Science and Engineering, Manipal Institute of Technology (MIT),
Manipal Academy of Higher Education (MAHE), Manipal, India
[3] Forensic Medicine, Kasturba Medical College (KMC), Manipal Academy of Higher
Education (MAHE), Manipal, India
{kkp.prakash,srikanth.prabhu,vinod.nayak}@manipal.edu

Abstract. Face Recognition System (FRS) is a significant area for communicating non verbally in day-to-day life. It is well understood that the face is a unique and vital part of the human body in identifying a person. Therefore, it can be used to identify faces for commercial and law enforcement applications. The aim of this study is to explore the relationship of facial proportion with respect to golden ratio for identifying a person. The goal of this paper is to investigate the application of divine proportions among human faces to extract features for classification and recognition using an ensemble classifier model. These feature extraction techniques can be used in image analysis, the advantages of which can be used for commercial purposes and criminal investigation processes.

Keywords: Facial images · Image ratio · Golden ratio · Ensemble learning · Forensics

1 Introduction

Bio-metric signatures rely on the consideration that each individual is unique. In determining the physical appearance, the face is the most significant individual factor. Recognizing a face is a natural ability of human vision. Facial recognition being a category of biometric identification is used in place of other biometric modalities when not available. Face capturing being natural and non-intrusive has conclusively become one of the best bio-metrics for face recognition. Computer vision has tried to resemble the ability of human vision with no conclusive performance. The most remarkably available identification systems in forensic

Supported by Manipal Institute of Technology, Manipal Academy of Higher Education (MAHE), Manipal, India.

science are DNA identification and fingerprint. However, face recognition stands to be a worthy and practical tool used by forensic examiners for criminal investigation.

Facial recognition in forensics deals with recognizing facial images in non ideal and unconstrained environment such as illumination, facial pose, expression, and occlusion variation. The recognition performance is highly impacted by the aforementioned conditions. This paper focus on techniques and algorithm to differentiate the similar faces and identical twins. Hence it is very challenging in recognizing similar faces, twins, the same person of different ages, etc. The study focuses on algorithms and techniques to distinguish between similar faces. This study propose a new data-set for checking facial differentiation for similar face classification. Each face image, identification is done Using various possible ratios. The study proposes a new measure of evaluation for face recognition algorithms by exploring the property of golden ratio in a human face and using ensemble classifier model for decision making. The primary motivation is to create an accurate system of face recognition that imitates the forensic examiners' method to precisely determine the identity of similar faces involved in criminal activities.

1.1   Statement of the Problem

There is incredible increase in the number of criminals and crime rate, which is a great concern for law enforcement and hence prevention of crime and criminal identification has become a primary need. As of today, criminal offenses appear to be committed by similar looking people at a high rate. Recent researchers have revealed that the face recognition system does not perform exceptionally in the case of similar faces. Therefore, when utilizing any bio-metric tools for identification, mistaken identifications mustn't take place to avoid accidentally holding an innocent person guilty.

The case history of such crimes is presented below as follows:

- According to [1], in 2003, the Kuala Lumpur police in Malaysia, apprehended a man driving a car carrying drugs to his house where his twin brother was also present and detained as well. In Malaysia, drug trafficking is a serious crime that attracts capital punishment, the case was heard in court after six years, where the DNA test offered by the police as evidence could not identify the twins and therefore the judge had to release both the twins.

- In January 2009, in Berlin, Germany, a luxury department store was broken into by a group of thieves who got away with jewelry and watches worth $6.5 million. Police found implicating DNA evidence through their sweat samples matching one of the identical twins. Suspecting that one of them have engaged in the crime, the police detained both the twins. They had to set them free since the identical twins could not be identified exactly.

- According to [1] in 2009, the Nigerian security forces have repeatedly declared that the Boko Haram leader -Abubakar Shekau had been killed. Less than a year later videos were posted on the internet that the warlord leader Abubakar Shekau was alive. In other words, an assumed innocent man has been killed mistaken for Shekau. (Mistaken identity).
- At the end of 2012, six women were raped in Marseille France. The Evidence which included the DNA test guided the police to arrest two suspects (Elwin and Yohan) who were identical twins. The victims recognized the twins but were unable to exactly identify the one who assaulted them, as reported.
- On February 12, 2011, A suspect was held by the police within a month for a murder that occurred in Arizona. One of the twin brothers was found to be a suspect responsible for the murder. The case came to premature closure since the Biometric Verification was not good enough to implicate the suspect.

The identification of similar or look alike faces pose a challenge and holds a good reason for pursuing their recognition.

The solution to this challenge can be debated based on the golden ratio.

- "The golden ratio" sometimes called the "divine proportion" is a mathematical expression of the divine creation because of its frequency in the manifestation of any type of form in the natural world. Hence any form and its features with its various proportions may be compared with this single divine golden ratio as a benchmark measurement to differentiate.

The aforementioned problem and reason with regards to the golden ratio to scan distinctive regions of the face for identification motivates and inspires well to work on developing a new integrated system where a significant region of the face is hunted on similar faces used for matching, which can be a solution with high accuracy.

It has been observed that the existing face recognition system does not effectively identify identical twins. It is a challenge in face recognition even for deep neural network to distinguish between identical twins using their face images as mentioned in [27,28] and [2]. Hence the main significance of the proposed study is to determine authentic identification of similar faces such as Look-alike and identical twins engaged in committing forensic related fraud and crime.

Until now the concept of golden ratio has been used for face detection, face shape analysis, beautification, plastic surgery etc. Recently there is evidence of using this concept in face recognition for door access control and criminal identification using face sketch image.

Also according to [3] face curve is the most distinctive region in differentiating between similar faces mainly identical twins. However there is not much work done on analysing the face curve. There is a need to focus more on face curve analysis with respect to local features such that the rate at which the face curve changes with respect to the angle subtended at a point of the determined local feature. Hence the proposed approach uses the concept of image ratio and golden ratio in analysing the face curve with respect to the local features for its application in forensics, intending to mimic the forensic examiners way of facial comparison. It could be then able to present strong statistical evidence of meaningful value to support the forensic expert in the court, which is acceptable by the judicial system.

2 Literature Survey and Related Work

This section reviews the existing literature based on identical twin-face recognition systems. The review significantly focuses on works that discuss forensic aspects and their applications in face recognition. Identification of Identical twins poses a considerable challenge due to unique similarities in features occurring in twins. The various methods and approaches for the identification of twins are summarized as follows:

Bio-metric techniques can differentiate similar faces, and this makes the technique a subject of interest as mentioned in [4]. The literature survey has been reviewed and evaluated for the efficiency of existing face recognition systems in identifying human faces more so in similar faces. The summary of the literature survey with relevant citations quoted that has paved the way to explore and propose a new method as expressed below.

Face recognition techniques are used in many fields and significantly in forensic sciences [1] to recognize criminals. Face recognition being a popular scientific technique with its enormous application is also vulnerable to many challenges as mentioned by [5,6] and [7]. Humans are naturally trained to recognize each face's unique imprint through their distinctive features. It is this capability of human vision in measuring a face for identification, that has been explored in face recognition. Thus, a lot of attention is drawn towards developing algorithms that duplicate the process of human vision for face recognition. In the research survey, the crime related to similar faces has been highlighted and relevant topics related to the forensic investigation with procuring of statistical evidence to be presented in the court of law which is mentioned in [8] and [1].

A Face recognition system consists of face detection, pre-processing, landmark detection, feature extraction, feature selection, classification, identification, and authentication. The literature refers to face image analysis using the image ratios and golden ratios as mentioned in [9,23,24,26], and [10]. The golden ratio-based feature extraction approach is inspired by the reasoning of human vision's capability in viewing significant features of the whole face, which according to [3] face curve is the most distinctive region in differentiating between similar faces mainly identical twins. However, there is not much work done on analysing the face curve for recognition.

Until now the concept of golden ratio [10,11] has been used for face detection [14], feature section [13,29], face shape analysis [12,15], beautification [16], plastic surgery etc. Recently there is evidence of using this concept very sparsely in face recognition for door access control [17] and criminal identification using face sketch image [18]. The literature review further discusses various Machine learning classifier/Ensemble classifiers such as [25], and [19] such as SVM as mentioned by [20], KNN, Bayesian Net as proposed by [21], etc. along with their merits and demerits.

It has been observed that the existing face recognition system does not effectively identify identical twins. It is a challenge in face recognition even for deep neural network to distinguish between identical twins using their face images as mentioned in [2] and [22].

This study is categorically focused on exploring forensic aspects and the applications of the biometric face recognition system.

3   Methodology

This study aims to propose a novel framework that can provide a perfect matching decision for the identification of similar faces.

Overview of the Proposed Approach
Initially, from the data set, a face image is selected. Every chosen image of the data-set undergoes pre-processing for detection and normalization of the face.

The proposed system is used to automatically localize accurate landmarks and perform feature extraction using anthropometric measurements for face image analysis based on golden ratio and image ratio taken about the face curve concerning the local features, the results of which will be given to ensemble classifier such as KNN, Random Forest, SVM and Logistic regression for classifying same faces (Look alike faces) and different faces to enhance the accuracy of the face recognition system.

To conclude with performance evaluation, the performance results of this framework will be evaluated for its accuracy, error rate, recall, precision, and F-measure. The important aim of the system is to accomplish low complexity, high accuracy, and speedy identification by developing very efficient algorithms with the maximum possible similar face detection.

The process could be decomposed into four stages namely Face detection, Pre-processing and Landmark detection, Feature Extraction, and Classification as shown in Fig. 1.

1. **Face detection**: It is to identify a human face in an image. Since the identified results are dependent on numerous factors like environment, illumination, movement, orientation, and facial expressions it is challenging to detect the face in images.
2. **Pre-processing and Landmark Detection**: Facial image is captured and then pre-processed to procure "clean" faces. The selected image undergoes pre-processing for detection of and normalizing each face.
   Landmark detection allows a reliable and accurate identification of landmarks of the face. The proposed system is used to automatically localize accurate landmarks and perform feature extraction. Few definite points called landmark points have to be plotted on the individual facial images to get the needed measurements.

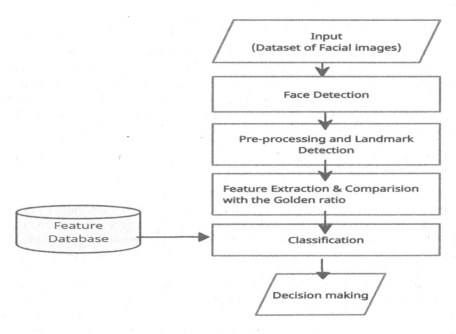

Fig. 1. Workflow of the proposed method.

3. **Feature extraction and comparison:** The process of extracting digital details, figures, or particulars from the raw data is called "Feature Extraction". The extracted features contain only discriminatory information. The feature extracting process will be carried out by using euclidean distance for already located anthropometric points and then various ratios are measured and compared with the golden ratio to find the discriminatory information which is considered as extracted features.

4. **Classification:** The process of sorting out data into labeled classes by a classifier, which is an algorithm, is called Classification. Here multiple classifiers such as SVM, Bayesian, KNN, Decision Tree, and Logistic Regression etc. will be used to learn the discriminatory features that supports and improves forensic investigation.

5. **Performance Evaluation:** The proposed system will get tested and also evaluated by using the self created data-set from the Forensic Medicine and Toxicology laboratory.

4   Research Methods

Following are the methods carried out to test the feasibility of the proposed plan designed. The details of the data sets required in the proposed method are expressed below.

4.1 Data Collection and Validation

The collection of data will be drawn from many sources. Few of the data that has been considered and some of them that are planned to be used for the study are mentioned here. Study supported by creating a database that contains a balanced set of 500 images of celebrities and photographs of Indian faces from the department of Forensic Medicine and Toxicology laboratory which contains individual faces of male and female, look-alikes etc.

4.2 Background Theory

In the face recognition researcher community, the typical understanding is that distinguishing between similar faces like Look-alikes and especially Identical twins is the most demanding and difficult problem in face recognition. Biometric print derived from the faces of identical twins is very similar. Remarkable approaches with the best of algorithms and databases have been presented over the years considering the favorable and unfavorable situation to study face recognition and have been found unsuccessful in matching up to expectations. With the increased birth rate of identical twins and they being the cause for fraud and growing crime rate, there is an increased urgency and need to integrate the existing automated face recognition system with forensic face recognition method which has an immense liability to follow legal procedures.

4.3 Face Anthropometry

Anthropometry is the scientific study of the measurements and proportions of the human body. Morphometry refers to the quantitative analysis of size and shape which is the fusion of geometry and biology dealing with the study of forms in two or threedimensional space. In the 18th century Alphonge Bertillon a French police officer and bio-metrics researcher generated a revolutionary system applying the anthropological technique of anthropometry for criminal identification, on the basis of which face recognition system exists.

Face Anthropometric evaluation begins with the identification of particular locations on a subject, called landmark points. Landmarks are localized automatically by importing Dlib package in Python executed through Visual Studio Code together with the Power-Shell extension. Table 1 provides the definitions for the same. The face detector is the method that locates the face of a human in an image and returns it as a bounding box or rectangle box value.

Table 1. Definition of anthropometry landmarks.

Anthropometry landmarks	Definition
Exocanthion (Ex)	The soft tissue point located at the outer commissure of eye fissure
Endocanthion (En)	The soft tissue point located at the inner commissure of eye fissure
Cheilion (Ch)	The point of the mouth corner
Stomion (Sto)	The midpoint of the labial commissure when the lips are closed
Gnathion (Gn)	The lowest median landmark on the lower border of the mandible
Trichion (Tr)	Anterior hairline at the mid-line
Pogonion (Pg)	The most anterior midpoint of the chin
Glabella (G)	The most prominent midline between eyebrows
Nasion (N)	The midpoint on the soft tissue contour of the base of the nasal root
Subnasale (Sn)	Junction of the inferior portion of the nasal septum and the upper lip
Pronasale (Prn)	The most anterior midpoint of the nasal tip
Pogonion (Pg)	The most anterior midpoint of the chin

After detecting the face position in an image, the next process is to locate the landmarks. The Dlib's 68 points facial landmark detection model shows all the required points of a human face. Sample anthropometry landmarks on the face are shown in Fig. 2.

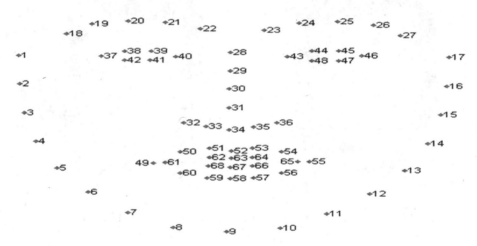

Fig. 2. Sixty-eight facial landmarks obtained by the Dlib facial landmark predictor.

Using this model, a total of 68 landmarks were acquired as important features and inter-landmark length measurements were then collected.

The Fig. 3 below shows results of face detection and landmarks detection for an individual face. The Fig. 4 below shows results of face detection and landmarks detection for Look-alike face.

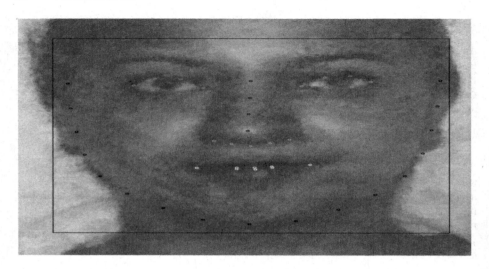

Fig. 3. Face detection and Sixty-eight facial landmarks detection.

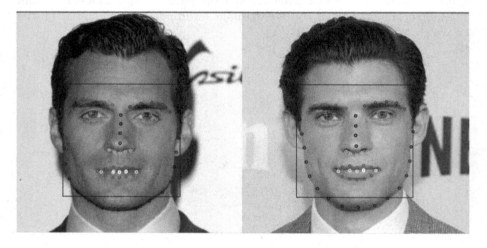

Fig. 4. Face detection and Sixty-eight facial landmarks detection- Look-Alike.

4.4   Feature Extraction

Feature extraction can be accomplished manually or automatically. Here various distances are measured such as left eyebrow width, right eyebrow width, left eye width, right eye width, mouth width, nose width, eyes width, left nose height, right nose height, lips height, chin height, nose to mouth, mouth height, left eye height, right eye height etc.

The below Fig. 5 shows the extraction of facial features using Euclidean distances from a single face.

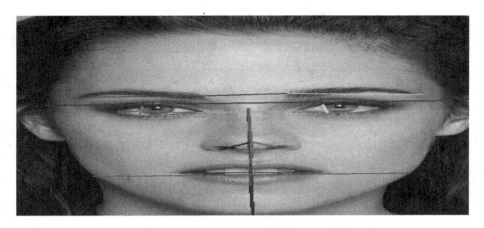

Fig. 5. Feature extraction using Euclidean distance -Individual face.

The below Fig. 6 shows the feature Extraction using Euclidean distance from similar faces.

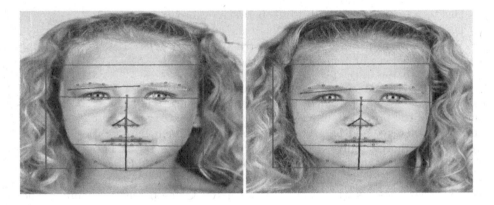

Fig. 6. Feature extraction using Euclidean distance -Identical twins.

4.5   Facial Image Analysis Using Golden Ratio and Image Ratio

The golden ratio sometimes called the "divine proportion," is a mathematical expression of the divine creation because of its frequency in the manifestation of any type of form in the natural world which is used here as benchmark for reference. Hence any form and its features with its various proportions may be compared with this single divine golden ratio as a benchmark measurement.

4 The Fig. 7 illustrate the geometric definition.

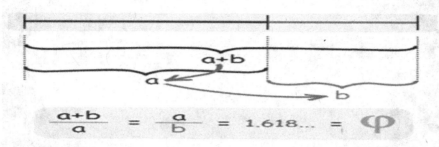

$$\frac{a+b}{a} = \frac{a}{b} = 1.618... = \varphi$$

Fig. 7. Illustration regarding the Definition of the Golden ratio.

Following are some of the golden ratios in the human face.

- Length of face/width of face
- Length of mouth/width of nose
- Distance between pupils/distance between eyebrows
- Distance between the lips and where the eyebrows meet/length of the nose
- Width of nose/distance between nostrils
- Distance between lip-chin/width of the nose
- Distance between the eyes/width of the nose

Along with these above-mentioned ratios there are additional image ratios included in the proposed approach. "The golden ratio" is used here as a benchmark for reference and hence one can compare different image ratios obtained vertically or horizontally with the value of the golden ratio. These ratios are then calculated as the percentage value of the golden ratio. Here, various ratios are measured by considering vertical-vertical measurements and horizontal-horizontal measurements which are then calculated as the percentage value of the golden ratio. In addition to horizontal and vertical ratios, ratios along the face curve with respect to the local feature were determined. These ratios were then compared with the golden ratio.

Figures 8 and 9 show golden ratio and image ratio-based facial image and facial curve analysis using already extracted anthropometry landmark points. By considering the points on the face curve and other landmark points one can measure the various ratios.

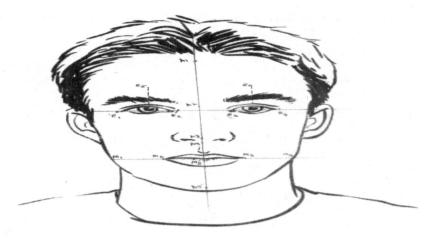

Fig. 8. Facial image analysis using golden ratio.

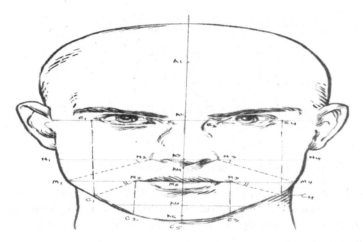

Fig. 9. Face curve analysis by measuring ratios

Twelve sample ratios which can be compared with the golden ratio for facial image analysis are as shown here. Using the aforementioned measurements, in all total 35 ratios are considered to compare with the phi ratio for facial image analysis.

Table 2. Facial image analysis using various ratios to compare with the golden ratio

$$Ratio_1 : (A2, A5; A2, A3) = \frac{A2 \cdot A5}{A2 \cdot A3} \tag{1}$$

$$Ratio_2 : (E1, E4; M2, M3) = \frac{E1 \cdot E4}{M2 \cdot M3} \tag{2}$$

$$Ratio_3 : (E1, E4; E1, E3) = \frac{E1 \cdot E4}{E2 \cdot E3} \tag{3}$$

$$Ratio_4 : (E1, E4; E2, E4) = \frac{E1 \cdot E4}{E2 \cdot E4} \tag{4}$$

$$Ratio_5 : (E1, C1; M2, C2) = \frac{E1 \cdot C1}{M2 \cdot C2} \tag{5}$$

$$Ratio_6 : (E2, C4; M3, C3) = \frac{E2 \cdot C4}{M3 \cdot C3} \tag{6}$$

$$Ratio_7 : (A2, C5; E4, C4) = \frac{A2 \cdot C5}{E4 \cdot C4} \tag{7}$$

$$Ratio_8 : (M1, M4; M1, M3) = \frac{M1 \cdot M4}{M1 \cdot M3} \tag{8}$$

$$Ratio_9 : (M1, M4; M2, M4) = \frac{M1 \cdot M4}{M2 \cdot M4} \tag{9}$$

$$Ratio_10 : (M1, M3; M1, M5) = \frac{M1 \cdot M3}{M1 \cdot M5} \tag{10}$$

$$Ratio_11 : (M4, M2; M4, M5) = \frac{M4 \cdot M2}{M4 \cdot M5} \tag{11}$$

$$Ratio_12 : (E11, E22; E12, E21) = \frac{E11 \cdot E22}{E12 \cdot E21} \tag{12}$$

4.6   Classification Using Ensemble Learning Model

A machine learning technique known as an ensemble method make use of the combined predictions from many other machine learning models (base models/estimators) into one predictive model. Thereby producing very accurate predictions than using any single model to improve the overall performance. Here in ensemble methods, a number of number of ML algorithms like SVM, KNN, Decision Tree, Random Forest, Extra tree classifier and Logistics Regression, etc. are combined together to seek the prediction. The block diagram of the ensemble learning model used in this paper is shown in Fig. 10 below.

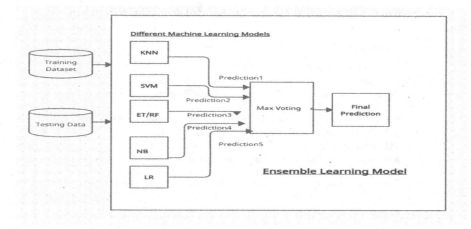

Fig. 10. Block diagram of the ensemble learning model.

4.7 Implementation Details

The algorithms are implemented with the Python 3.8 in VS code framework and power shell window. For automated face detection and landmark detection, existing models which is available in OpenCV, Dlib is used. Algorithms 1 and 2 explain the feature extraction and classification process of the proposed approach.

Algorithm 1: Feature extraction process

Procedure Extractor:

1. Initialization:
   points_array = [collection of points that we need to calculate ratios of]
2. **if** index.csv not generated
   Call build_index
   else
   Data ← get_data_from('extractor_input.csv')
   end if
3. diffs = []
4. **for each row in data:**
   diff = []
   ratioA ← get_ratios_from_index(row['source_img'])
   ratioB ←get_ratios_from_index(row['target_img'])
   diff. append (abs (ratioA - ratioB))
   diff. append (row['classification'])
   diffs. append(diff)
5. store (diffs, 'extractor_output.csv')
   end **for**
   end **Procedure**

Algorithm 2: Ensemble Learning model for Classification

Procedure Ensemble:

1. data <- open('extractor_output.csv')
2. same_lookalike_data <- drop_rows_with_lookalike(data)
3. same_different_data <- drop_rows_with_lookalike(data)

4. M1=apply neighbors. KNeighbors Classifier (same_lookalike_data)
5. M2=apply svm.SVC Classifier (same_lookalike_data)
6. M3=apply tree. Extra Tree Classifier (same_lookalike_data)
7. M4=apply Naïve Bayes Classifier (same_lookalike_data)
8. M5=apply Logistic Regression Classifier (same_lookalike_data)
9. Final Model= apply ensemble. Voting Classifier (M1, M2, M3, M4, M5)
10. Calculate accuracy_score for individual classifier and Ensemble learning model
11. Print confusion_matrix

12. M1=apply neighbors. KNeighbors Classifier (same_different_data)
13. M2=apply svm.SVC Classifier (same_different_data)
14. M3=apply RandomForestClassifier (same_different_data)
15. M4=apply Naïve Bayes Classifier (same_different_data)
16. M5=apply Logistic Regression Classifier (same_different_data)
17. Final Model= apply ensemble. Voting Classifier (M1, M2, M3, M4, M5)
18. Calculate accuracy_score for individual classifier and Ensemble learning model
19. Print confusion_matrix
end Procedure

5   Experimental Results

Classification result is obtained from the ensemble learning model using KNN, SVM, Random Forest and Logistic Regression that has been tested by using self-created data-set.

Tables below show the comparison of results tested between the various machine learning algorithms as mentioned above on the confusion matrix. The final result is a comparison of model classification to see which algorithm has the best accuracy and improves the performance of the model.

Table 3 shows the comparison of the classification model accuracy obtained for similar faces (Look-Alike). Model ensemble accuracy is (74%) which can be further increased by considering more number of images for comparison of similar faces.

Table 3. Classification accuracy comparison for similar faces

KNN	SVM	Extra Tree	Naive Bayes	Logistic Regression
70%	71%	74%	73%	72%

Figure 11 shows the comparison graph of the classification accuracy for the similar faces.

The Extra tree classifier model is the best classification model which gives the best accuracy to predict similar faces (74%) compared to KNN (70%), SVM (71%), Naive Bayes (73%) and Logistic Regression (72%).

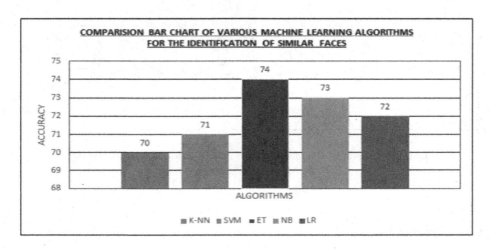

Fig. 11. Comparison of the classification accuracy for similar faces.

Table 4 shows the comparison of the classification model obtained for same/different faces. Fig. 12 shows the graph of comparison of the classification accuracy for the same/different faces.

Table 4. Classification accuracy comparison for same/different faces

KNN	SVM	Random Forest	Naive Bayes	Logistic Regression
82%	82%	84%	85%	80%

The Naive Bayes classifier model is the best classification model which gives the best accuracy to predict different faces (85%) compared to KNN (82%), SVM (82%), Random Forest (84%) and Logistic Regression (80%).

Model ensemble accuracy is (85%) which can be further increased by considering more number of images for comparison of different faces.

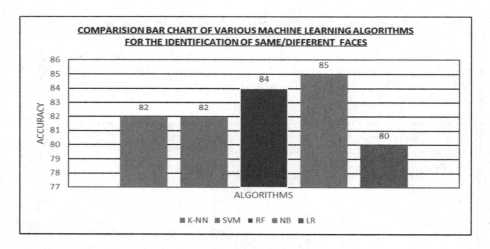

Fig. 12. Comparison of the classification accuracy for same/different faces.

6 Conclusion

From the golden ratio concept, the relationships between various ratios with respect to facial features and face curve is effectively analyzed. Further, the ensemble learning classifier such as SVM, Random forest etc. is used to recognize different categories of faces such as same, look-alikes, and different faces more so to be applicable in criminals identification. With the results obtained from this approach it can be concluded that out of five machine learning algorithms, SVM and Logistic regression gives the best performance in terms of accuracy. In future work, face recognition for identical twins can be considered, which is an open challenge still existing.

References

1. Chijindu, A.T., Chinagolum, I.: Machine learning based digital recognition of identical twins to support global crime investigation. Int. J. Latest Technol. Eng. Manag. Appl. Sci. (IJLTEMAS) (2018)
2. Ahmad, B., et al.: Deep convolutional neural network using triplet loss to distinguish the identical twins. In: 2019 IEEE Globecom Workshops (GC Wkshps). IEEE (2019)
3. Mousavi, S., Charmi, M., Hassanpoor, H.: Recognition of identical twins based on the most distinctive region of the face: human criteria and machine processing approaches. Multimedia Tools Appl. **80**(10), 15765–15802 (2021). https://doi.org/10.1007/s11042-020-10360-3
4. Rustam, Z., Faradina, R.: Face recognition to identify look-alike faces using support vector machine. J. Phys. Conf. Ser. **1108**(1) (2018)

5. Kukharev, G.A., Kaziyeva, N.: Digital facial anthropometry: application and implementation. Pattern Recogn. Image Anal. **30**(3), 496–511 (2020). https://doi.org/10.1134/S1054661820030141
6. Moung, E.G., et al.: Face recognition state-of-the-art, enablers, challenges and solutions: a review. Int. J. Adv. Trends Comput. Sci. Eng. **9**, 96–105 (2020)
7. Taskiran, M., Kahraman, N., Erdem, C.E.: Face recognition: past, present and future (a review). Digital Signal Process. **106**, 102809 (2020)
8. Prema, R., Shanmugapriya, P.: A review: face recognition techniques for differentiate similar faces and twin faces. In: 2017 International Conference on Energy, Communication, Data Analytics and Soft Computing (ICECDS). IEEE (2017)
9. Dhimar, T., Mistree, K.: Feature extraction for facial age estimation: a survey. In: 2016 International Conference on Wireless Communications, Signal Processing and Networking (WiSPNET). IEEE (2016)
10. Anand, S., et al.: Vertical and horizontal proportions of the face and their correlation to phi among Indians in Moradabad population: a survey. J. Indian Prosthodont. Soc. **15**(2), 125 (2015)
11. Hwang, K., Park, C.Y.: The divine proportion: origins and usage in plastic surgery. Plast. Reconstr. Surg. Glob. Open **9**(2), e3419 (2021)
12. Jan, N., et al.: Identification of facial shape by applying golden ratio in ethnic Kashmiri population
13. Dey, A., et al.: A hybrid meta-heuristic feature selection method using golden ratio and equilibrium optimization algorithms for speech emotion recognition. IEEE Access **8**, 200953–200970 (2020)
14. Hassaballah, M., Murakami, K., Ido, S.: Face detection evaluation: a new approach based on the golden ratio. Signal Image Video Process. **7**(2), 307–316 (2013)
15. Alam, M.K., et al.: Multiracial facial golden ratio and evaluation of facial appearance. PloS One **10**(11), e0142914 (2015)
16. Milutinovic, J., Zelic, K., Nedeljkovic, N.: Evaluation of facial beauty using anthropometric proportions. Sci. World J. **2014** (2014)
17. Gaikwad, P.S., Kulkarni, V.B.: Face Recognition Using Golden Ratio for Door Access Control System. Advances in Signal and Data Processing, pp. 209–231. Springer, Singapore (2021)
18. Ounachad, K.: Golden ratio and its application to Bayes classifier based face sketch gender classification and recognition (2020)
19. Dong, X., et al.: A survey on ensemble learning. Front. Comput. Sci. **14**(2), 241–258 (2020)
20. Vengatesan, K., et al.: Face recognition of identical twins based on support vector machine classifier. In: 2019 Third International conference on I-SMAC (IoT in Social, Mobile, Analytics and Cloud) (I-SMAC). IEEE (2019)
21. Vinay, A., et al.: Unconstrained face recognition using Bayesian classification. Procedia Comput. Sci. **143**, 519–527 (2018)
22. Rodriguez, M., Andrea, Z.G., Worring, M.: Likelihood ratios for deep neural networks in face comparison. J. Forensic Sci. **65**(4), 1169–1183 (2020)
23. Packiriswamy, V., Kumar, P., Rao, M.: Identification of facial shape by applying golden ratio to the facial measurements: an interracial study in Malaysian population. N. Am. J. Med. Sci. **4**(12), 624 (2012)
24. Alsawwaf, M., et al.: In your face: person identification through ratios and distances between facial features. Vietnam J. Comput. Sci. 1–16 (2021)
25. Hamayun, A.K.: Feature fusion and classifier ensemble technique for robust face recognition. Signal Process. Int. J. **11**, 1–15 (2017)

26. Bao, Y., Yin, Y., Musa, L.: Face recognition and using ratios of face features in gender identification. In: Proceedings of the International Conference on Image Processing, Computer Vision, and Pattern Recognition (IPCV). The Steering Committee of The World Congress in Computer Science, Computer Engineering and Applied Computing (WorldComp) (2015)

27. Rehkha, K.K., Vinod, V.: A literary survey on multimodal biometric identification of monozygotic twins. In: Komanapalli, V.L.N., Sivakumaran, N., Hampannavar, S. (eds.) Advances in Automation, Signal Processing, Instrumentation, and Control. LNEE, vol. 700, pp. 385–398. Springer, Singapore (2021). https://doi.org/10.1007/978-981-15-8221-9_36

28. Mohammed, B.O.: A multimodal biometric system using global features for identical twins identification. Int. J. Trends Comput. Sci. **14**, 92–107 (2018)

29. Sudhakar, K.., Nithyanandam, P..: Facial identification of twins based on fusion score method. J. Ambient Intell. Humaniz. Comput. 1–12 (2021). https://doi.org/10.1007/s12652-021-03012-3

Anomaly and Intrusion Detection

Detecting Anomalies in Natural Gas Production: A Boosting Tree Based Model

Sibo Yang[1], Zhenjia Wang[2], Liping Liu[2], Yang Liu[2], Hu Chen[2], and Xichen Tang[3(✉)]

[1] China University of Petroleum, Beijing, China
sbyang@tulip.academy
[2] The first gas production plant of Changqing Oilfield Branch, Xi'an, China
{wzj_cq,liulp001_cq,liuy03_cq,chenh1_cq}@petrochina.com.cn
[3] Qingdao University of technology, Qingdao, China

Abstract. Natural gas is one of the important energy sources. However, during the production process of natural gas, abnormal events often occurred due to various factors so that the pumping equipment could not work. At present, the detection of abnormal production of gas wells mainly relies on the personal experience of engineers. The continuous production of gas well data puts huge pressure on limited manpower. Moreover, the results of manual judgment are often unreliable due to personal subjectivity, and problems such as failure to find abnormalities in time. The objective of this paper is to establish a fast and reliable data-driven anomaly detection framework. Its focus is managing and processing a high volume of data to improve operational efficiency, enhance decision making and mitigate risks in the workplace. The proposed framework employs a state-of-the-art algorithm, called boosting tree, which can not only identify point anomalies but also find context anomalies based on historical data. Comparing the test results with the manual annotation results on several real gas production datasets, the results show that the proposed framework is proficient at detecting anomalies.

Keywords: Natural gas · Anomaly detection · Boosting tree

1 Introduction

Natural gas is one of the important energy sources [19]. It has been widely used in transportation [17], chemical industry [4]. In actual gas production, gas wells often have low productivity. However, the low gas production of such wells is not due to the small natural gas reserves, but is affected by various factors such as fluid accumulation and blockage in the production process, so that the production capacity is suppressed.

Figure 1 shows the actual production data of a gas well, from which it can be seen that a large number of abnormal gas production events occur in the production process. The production environment of gas well is very complex, and

© Springer Nature Singapore Pte Ltd. 2022
S. R. Pokhrel et al. (Eds.): ATIS 2021, CCIS 1554, pp. 83–95, 2022.
https://doi.org/10.1007/978-981-19-1166-8_7

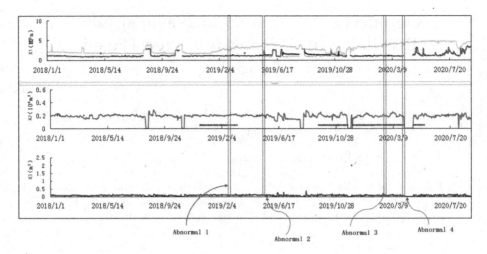

Fig. 1. Gas production curve of a gas well.

its anomalies are often caused by multiple reasons. If anomalies can be detected and processed in time when they occur, unplanned or unnecessary system maintenance can be avoided. Otherwise, it may lead to very bad machine failures, resulting in a large number of manpower and material losses.

At present, the abnormal detection of gas wells mainly relies on engineers to judge according to their own experience [18]. Engineers monitor the production indicators of gas wells and get some rules for detecting abnormal production based on their own experience. It requires engineers to continuously monitor the production status of gas wells and take corresponding measures for different gas wells. The count of experienced engineers is limited but the production data of gas wells are constantly generated. A large number of gas wells produce data at the same time, which not only causes a significant increase in the requirement of manpower but also makes it difficult to detect anomalies. In addition, the judgment method based on personal experience will lead to inaccurate results due to the influence of personal subjectivity.

This work aims to enhance the ability to detect abnormal events in production by introducing Machine Learning (ML) techniques for anomaly detection in the gas production process. In the last decades, ML has been utilized in a great variety of areas such as industrial [15, 23], social media [22], and economic activities. Anomaly detection is an important area of Machine Learning, which aims to detect abnormal data that is significantly different from previously observed observations. It has been employed for detecting any abnormal events such as intrusion detection [10], fraud detection [7], event detection in social networks [2].

In this work, we propose an anomaly detection framework for gas well production, which will be used to quickly detect abnormal events in gas production. Detection of anomalies in gas well production is challenging, mainly because:

1. The features related to gas well anomalies must be identified and separated;
2. The data generated by gas wells are large and are greatly affected by the conditions of gas wells;

The proposed framework aims to overcome these challenges and provides usable anomalies detection systems.

The contribution of this work can be summarized as follows :

– This is the first gas well production anomaly detection framework based on machine learning in literature;
– To the best of our knowledge, this is the first abnormal event in the literature that applies boosting technology to detect gas well production;
– Experiments on the actual production data of several gas wells show that the proposed framework has high accuracy.

The rest of the paper is organized as follows: gas well anomaly and its principles are described in Sect. 2. In Sect. 3 the proposed anomaly detection framework is presented with a brief review of the employed anomaly detection methods. Experimental settings and results are detailed in Sect. 4; Finally, conclusive and future works are discussed in Sect. 5.

2   Related Work

2.1   Detection of Abnormal Gas Production

The causes of abnormal gas production are diverse and complex [18]. It may be due to the unreasonable production system, which led to the premature precipitation of condensate, reverse condensation of the reservoir, water blocking, and blockage of the foam drainage emulsion and other reservoir pollution problems. Therefore, if an abnormality is detected as early as possible, reactive operations can be taken in time, for example, to check related equipment for gas extraction in a gas well to eliminate faults and stabilize production. If the abnormality cannot be detected in a timely and effective manner, it may cause equipment failure, decrease in gas production, and, in serious cases, may result in a reduction in the life of the gas well.

At present, the abnormal detection of gas well production mainly relies on the engineer's experience to make manual judgments [16,21]. However, this method that completely depends on the engineer's experience often results in great differences in the results due to the engineer's subjective judgment, and the judgment results do not have the actual production guidance function. In addition, if only manual judgment is relied on, as the well volume increases, labor costs will inevitably increase. Although some methods based engineer's experience have been proposed for the detection of gas well production anomalies, the methods proposed are not well adapted to the contextual anomalies. And because its defined anomaly detection algorithm can only identify existing abnormal patterns, it cannot adaptively adjust anomaly detection strategies based on actual production data.

2.2   Anomaly Detection in Machine Learning

There are many kinds of machine learning methods proposed to solve the problem of anomaly detection. The distance based anomaly detection assumes that anomalies are far away from other data samples. The distance between all pair of data samples is calculated using a distance function. A data sample is judged as anomalies when the distance between itself and others is large. The firstly distance-based method of anomaly detection is proposed in [12]. The K-neighbor distance is used to build the anomaly detector in [14,20]. After calculting the K-neighbor distance of each sample, the sample which have the largest distance are considered as anomalies. Although the distance-based method is easier to realize, the practical application of it is still limited since its time complexity is relatively high.

Anomalies are usually detected from an individual's point of view, i.e. the anomalies are far from their neighboring clusters. Therefore, it is not appropriate to use the overall distance as distance based methods do. The density-based anomaly detection algorithms are proposed to solve this problem. The Local Outlier Factor (LOF) [8] is proposed to detect anomalies by considering the local density of a data sample and its neighbors. If the local density of a data sample is much lower than that of its neighbors, this data object is considered as anomalier. Local parsimony factor (LCF) is proposed to reduce the complexity of the computation by adapting k nearset distance which is the maximum distance between the k nearest data samples [1]. The density-based method can detect local anomalies, and have high detection accuracy. However, the detecting accuracy of those algorithms is effect to their paprameter which are difficult to tune.

Because each model is specifically designed for different characteristics of perception. It is only applicable to certain aspects of the "whole truth". So it is best to integrate different third-party observational results to reach consensus. The main idea of this method (called "ensemble") is that if these judgments do not contain all the same errors. It is useful to combine individual judgments or the results of marginalized observations [24]. In this work, we adopt a ensemble method called boosting tree [9] to build abnormal detector. There are several reasons are considered: Firstly, due to its high performance in solving problems and the minimum requirements for feature engineering [5,6], it has been widely used in industry. Secoudly, compared with other algorithms such as deep learning algorithm, it is considered to be more easily obatained robust results in small data sets. Considering the limited size of dataset in this study, it is more suitable than other algorithms.

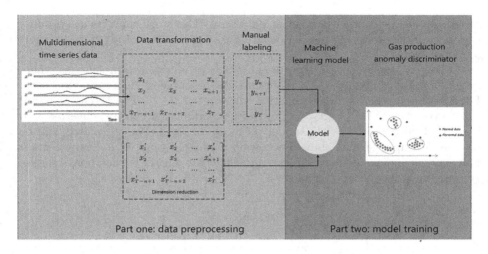

Fig. 2. Intelligent gas well anomaly detection framework.

3   Intelligent Anomaly Detection Framework

The purpose of gas well abnormality detection is to judge the current status of the gas well based on historical multiple variables, which is: input is the set of observed feature vectors $\{X\}_{t=1}^{T} = \{x_1, x_2, \cdots, x_T\}$ and the corresponding state $\{y\}_{t=1}^{T} = \{y_1, y_2, \cdots, y_T\}$. T is the length of the total time step, such as the number of days in the collected data set. The time step is t, y_t is the working state of the sample where $x_t \in R^m$. The gas well anomaly detection problem use multivariate $\{X\}_{t=1}^{T}$ and the time series of the gas well status $\{y\}_{t=1}^{T}$ as input to find a model f is constructed to judge the current gas well status y_{t+1}, namely:

$$\hat{y}_{T+1} = f\left(\{x_t\}_{t=1}^{T}, \{y_t\}_{t=1}^{T}\right) \tag{1}$$

Aiming at the characteristics of gas production data from gas wells, we establish a gas well anomaly detection framework as shown in Fig. 2. The framework is divided into two parts as a whole. The first part is the data preprocessing stage, including data conversion and feature extraction. The second part is the design and training of anomaly detection model.

3.1   Data Conversion

Gas well data is a kind of sequence data that changes over time. Only using the current time data cannot capture the influence of historical data on current decision-making, and it is impossible to judge the current abnormality through contextual information. Therefore, before designing the anomaly detection model, it is necessary to convert the gas production data in the form of time series into a time-context-dependent data form. This work converts gas production data in the form of time series into data in the form of input and output sequence pairs.

Let $X = \{x_1, x_2, \cdots, x_T\}$ represent T gas production data samples where $x_t \in R^m$ and $t \in \{1, 2, \cdots, T\}$, represents the t sample of gas production data. Let n represent the lag input quantity where $n \in 1, 2, \cdots, T-1$. The collected time series data $X = \{x_1, x_2, \cdots, x_T\}$ of gas production can be converted into the data form required by the model, as shown in Eq. 2. The left matrix will be used as the input of the anomaly detection model ($\{v_1, v_2, \cdots, v_n\}$ represents n independent independent variables), and the right matrix is the anomaly state (y represents dependent variables).

$$\begin{pmatrix} v_1 & v_2 & \cdots & v_n \\ x_1 & x_2 & \cdots & x_n \\ x_2 & x_3 & \cdots & x_{n+1} \\ \cdots & \cdots & \cdots & \cdots \\ x_{T-n} & x_{T-n+1} & \cdots & x_{T-1} \end{pmatrix} \rightarrow \begin{pmatrix} y \\ y_{n+1} \\ y_{n+2} \\ \cdots \\ y_T \end{pmatrix} \tag{2}$$

In a world, it uses the gas production data of the first n observation samples to judge the gas production state at the current time point.

3.2   Feature Extraction

Through the above-mentioned data conversion steps, the dimensionality of the input data is increased to $m \times n$, and the increase of the dimensionality is prone to dimensional disasters. A large amount of redundant information makes the model training difficult to converge and the training speed is reduced. We use the maximum information coefficient (MIC) [3] to filter the feature of high correlation so that the dimension is reduced to $m' \times n'$, where $m' \times n' < m \times n$. The retained features are maximized and remain independent of each other. Compared with the most commonly used Pearson correlation coefficient, MIC can overcome the limitation of maximum linearity and can find more relevant types of features.

We first briefly introduce the theory of mutual information as a prerequisite for understanding MIC. Let A and B indicates two random variables with discrete values. Mutual information is used to measure the decrease in uncertainty about the variable after observing anather variable, or measure the decrease in uncertainty after observing the variable through symmetry. It can be calculated by Eq. 3.

$$I(A; B) = \sum_{a \in A} \sum_{b \in B} p(a, b) \log \frac{p(a, b)}{p(a)p(b)} \tag{3}$$

According to Eq. 3, if $I(A; B) = 0$ then the variables A and B are independent; Otherwise, A and B has correlation. In this case, the larger the value of Mutual information is, the higher correlation between two variables.

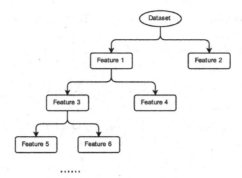

Fig. 3. Simple tree model.

Given two variables A and B and a finite data set $D = \{a_i, b_i\}$, where $|D| = n$, assuming that the A, B axes are divided into n_a, n_b bins, respectively. Let G represents obtained $n_a \times n_b$ grid. Then the probability distribution $D|_G$ can be approximatly calculated by the ratio of data points falling into grids.

Given a data set $D \in R^2$ and the grid $n_a \times n_b$, the maximum mutual information is defined as:

$$I^*(D, n_a, n_b) = \max I\left(D|_G\right) \tag{4}$$

where $I\left(D|_G\right)$ is the mutual information of the data set D under the gird G.

The elements of the characteristic matrix $M(D)$ of the data set D is defined as

$$M(D)_{n_a, n_b} = \frac{I^*(D, n_a, n_b)}{\log \min\{n_a, n_b\}} \tag{5}$$

where $\log \min\{n_a, n_b\}$ normalize all entities of the matrix $M(D)$ falls into the domain $[0, 1]$.

The MIC value of the data set $D(|D| = n)$ with two variables is defined as.

$$\text{MIC}(D) = \max_{n_a \times n_b \leq B(n)} \{M(D)_{n_a, n_b}\} \tag{6}$$

where default value $B(n) = n^{0.6}$.

Given the class label Y, the MIC value of each feature X can be calculated, all original features can be sorted according to their MIC values, and a subset of these features can be selected.

3.3 Boosting Tree

The mechanism of the boosting tree is keep adding and training multiple simple trees, as shown in Fig. 3, in a weighted manner to form a strong anomaly detector, thereby improving the detection effect.

$$y_i = f(x_i) = \sum_{k=1}^{K} f_k(x_i) \tag{7}$$

where K is the total number of trees, f_k is the Kth tree, and y_i is the prediction result of x_i.

The loss function of the model is defined as:

$$\text{Obj}(\theta) = \sum_{i=1}^{n} l\left(y_i, x_i\right) + \sum_{k=1}^{K} \Omega\left(f_k\right) \tag{8}$$

where $l(y_i, x_i)$ is the training loss of X samples, and $\Omega\left(f_k\right)$ is the regular term;

Regular items are defined as:

$$\Omega\left(f_k\right) = \alpha T + \frac{1}{2}\lambda \sum_{j=1}^{T} w_j^2 \tag{9}$$

where T is the total number of nodes in the tree model, w_j is the weight of corresponding leaf nodes, α and λ are constants and penalty coefficients; A leaf node is a node that has no children. The purpose of regular term is to control the complexity of the model and effectively prevent over fitting.

In order to solve the loss function, the Taylor expansion is obtained:

$$Obj^{(t)} \approx \sum_{i=1}^{n} \left[l\left(y_i, \hat{y}_i^{(t-1)}\right) + g_i f_t\left(x_i\right) + \frac{1}{2} h_i f_t^2\left(x_i\right) \right] + \Omega\left(f_t\right) \tag{10}$$

where $g_i = \partial_{\hat{y}}(t-1) l\left(y_i, \hat{y}^{(t-1)}\right)$, $h_i = \partial_{\hat{y}(t-1)}^2 l\left(y_i, \hat{y}^{(t-1)}\right)$.

During model training, the loss function can be expressed as:

$$Obj^{(t)} = \sum_{i=1}^{n} \left[\left(\sum_{i \in I_j} g_i\right) w_j + \frac{1}{2}\left(\sum_{i \in I_j} h_i + \lambda\right) w_j^2 \right] + \alpha T \tag{11}$$

where $I_j = \{i | q(x_i = j)\}$ is the feature set of classification nodes. The optimal solution of the function can be obtained by differentiating the loss function and solving the optimization conditions, namely:

$$W_j^* = \frac{G_j}{H_j + \lambda} \tag{12}$$

$$Obj = -\frac{1}{2} \sum_{j=1}^{T} \left(\frac{G_j^2}{H_j + \lambda} + \alpha T \right) \tag{13}$$

4   Experimental Results

4.1   Data Preparation

Due to device limitations and data availability, our datasets include six features as shown below:

- Working hour. Working hours of the day for a well.
- Tubing pressure. Tubing pressure is the residual pressure of oil and gas flowing from the bottom hole to the wellhead.
- Casing pressure. The pressure gauge for measuring casing pressure is connected with the annular space between the oil pipe and the casing. Its size reflects the annular space pressure and the amount of natural gas separated from the oil.
- Entrance pressure. Entrance pressure refers to the difference between the set pressure of the upstream station and the pressure loss in the midway.
- Daily gas production. Total daily gas production of gas wells.
- Daily water production. Total daily water production of gas wells.

The gas plant engineers have already manually labelled the anomalies for the four datasets. We have aligned all sensor features to the same timestamp over the available data collection periods. The original data characteristics of the 4 data sets are shown in Table 1. Each gas well has different anomaly rates and time series lengths.

Table 1. Description of gas well data.

Data set	Number of samples	Ratio of abnormalities	Data dimension
Gas well # 1	7406	0.07%	5
Gas well # 2	5306	4.41%	5
Gas well # 3	6339	5.68%	5
Gas well # 4	7403	10.44%	5

Verify the ability of the proposed framework to detect abnormalities on each gas production well through the following steps:

- Convert data into time series pair form;
- Use MIC for feature selection to remove features with MIC value greater than 0.8;
- By calculating the detection scores from all sample data, the ability of the detector to identify the abnormal state of the well is tested.

Then, repeat the above process with the data of the remaining wells in sequence. In the training model stage, 10-fold cross-validation [13] is used to adjust the parameters of the detector when needed.

4.2 Baseline

There are two rules of thumb used in the natural gas industry, provided by the engineers from the gas factory.

Table 2. Parameter value of daily water production

Daily water production(m^3/day)	Parameter n
[0,2)	2
(2,5]	1
(5,10]	0.8
(10,+∞]	0.5

1. The fluctuation of daily water production is a key condition to detect abnormal gas wells. If the daily water production in 3 d is higher than the n times average daily water production in the previous 10 d, it will consider the gas well abnormal. The value of n can be referred to Table 2.
2. If the casing pressure keeps rising during the working hours such that the average daily casing pressure is larger than that of the previous date, the gas well will be classified as abnormal.

4.3   Evaluation Measures

AUC is the most commonly used indicator to measure the effectiveness of methods in anomaly detection. AUC refers to the area under the ROC (receiver operating characteristic curve) curve [11]. ROC is a curve drawn based on a series of different thresholds, with the true positive rate as the ordinate and the false positive rate as the abscissa.

For the problem of abnormality detection, the false positive rate refers to the probability that it is judged to be abnormal but not really abnormal, that is, the probability that it is judged to be an abnormal case in a normal case. The true positive rate refers to the probability of being judged to be abnormal as well as being truly abnormal, that is, the probability of being judged to be abnormal in an abnormal case. The closer the AUC is, the higher the authenticity of the detection method; when it is equal, the authenticity is the lowest, and it has no application value.

4.4   Experimental Results

Figure 4 shows the ROC curve of the proposed framework on the data set. In an anomaly detector, the detection result is related to the preset threshold (greater than the threshold is 1, less than the threshold is 0). If the threshold is set to be very small, then more and more abnormal samples will be correctly judged. Then the true positive rate naturally rises, but at the same time, more and more normal samples are incorrectly predicted as abnormal, so the false positive rate also rises. As shown in Fig. 4, the framework proposed in this paper can predict the above abnormal samples when the horizontal axis value is relatively small.

Moreover, as shown in Table 3, our proposed model could effectively detect abnormalies overall gas wells. Even on gas well #1 with a small ratio of abnormalities, the model still performs well.

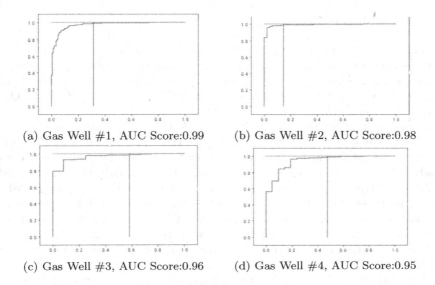

(a) Gas Well #1, AUC Score:0.99   (b) Gas Well #2, AUC Score:0.98

(c) Gas Well #3, AUC Score:0.96   (d) Gas Well #4, AUC Score:0.95

Fig. 4. AUC scores of ensemble tree algorithm on different datasets

Table 3. ROC-AUC values for different methods.

Methods	Gas well #1	Gas well #2	Gas well #3	Gas well #4
Conventional	0.54	0.54	0.53	0.51
Boosting tree	0.96	0.99	0.99	0.99

In addition, Fig. 5 shows the comparison between the predicted label of the framework proposed in this paper and the label of the expert on the data set. The results also show that the abnormal detection result of the proposed framework can well meet the manual labeling.

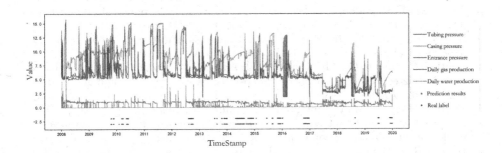

Fig. 5. Comparison of manual tags and model judgment tags.

5   Conclusion

Natural gas is one of the important energy sources. Gas well abnormality judgment occupies an important position in actual gas production. At present, in order to enable gas wells to engage in normal production, the detection of abnormal production of gas wells mainly relies on the investment of a large number of experienced engineers.

In this work, this paper proposes an intelligent gas well anomaly detection framework, which can not only greatly reduce the labor burden of gas production, but also intelligently detect context anomalies based on historical data. In particular, we use boosting tree to construct an anomaly detection model. The framework allows users to detect abnormal events in time. A preprocessing and feature extraction method is used in this framework, which is conducive to extracting features that determine anomalies. The framework proposed in this paper has been tested on several real gas well data sets with multiple abnormal rates. The results show that the framework has achieved good detection performance.

This study is the first step in enabling gas well production to self-detect its abnormal production. Our method can be applied to other devices with many different but interrelated modules. As a future research direction, we will study different types of anomalies and different types of anomaly detection algorithms in natural gas production.

References

1. Agyemang, M.: Algorithm for mining local outliers. In: Innovations Through Information Technology: 2004 Information Resources Management Association International Conference, New Orleans, Louisiana, USA, May 23–26, 2004. vol. 1, p. 5. IGI Global (2004)
2. Alallaq, N., Al-khiza'ay, M., Dohan, M.I., Han, X.: Sentiment analysis to enhance detection of latent astroturfing groups in online social networks. In: Chen, Q., Wu, J., Zhang, S., Yuan, C., Batten, L., Li, G. (eds.) ATIS 2018. CCIS, vol. 950, pp. 79–91. Springer, Singapore (2018). https://doi.org/10.1007/978-981-13-2907-4_7
3. Albanese, D., Riccadonna, S., Donati, C., Franceschi, P.: A practical tool for maximal information coefficient analysis. Oxford Open 7(4), giy032 (2018)
4. Lin, B., Wesseh, P.K., Jr.: Estimates of inter-fuel substitution possibilities in Chinese chemical industry. Energy Econ. 40(2), 560–568 (2013)
5. Bhati, B.S., Chugh, G., Al-Turjman, F., Bhati, N.S.: An improved ensemble based intrusion detection technique using xgboost. Trans. Emerg. Telecommun. Technol. 32(6), e4076 (2021)
6. Bhattacharya, S., Maddikunta, P.K.R., Kaluri, R., Singh, S., Gadekallu, T.R., Alazab, M., Tariq, U., et al.: A novel PCA-firefly based XGBoost classification model for intrusion detection in networks using GPU. Electronics 9(2), 219 (2020)
7. Bolton, R.J., Hand, D.J.: Statistical fraud detection: a review. Stat. Sci. 17(3), 235–249 (2002)
8. Breunig, M.M., Kriegel, H.P., NG, R.T., Sander, J.: Lof: identifying density-based local outliers. In: Proceedings of the 2000 ACM SIGMOD International Conference on Management of Data, pp. 93–104 (2000)

9. Chen, T., Guestrin, C.: Xgboost: a scalable tree boosting system. In: Proceedings of the 22nd ACM SIGKDD International Conference on Knowledge Discovery and Data Mining, pp. 785–794 (2016)
10. Garcia-Teodoro, P., Diaz-Verdejo, J., Maciá-Fernández, G., Vázquez, E.: Anomaly-based network intrusion detection: techniques, systems and challenges. Comput. Secur. **28**(1–2), 18–28 (2009)
11. Hanley, J.A., Mcneil, B.J.: The meaning and use of the area under a receiver operating characteristic (roc) curve. Radiology **143**(1), 29 (1982)
12. Knorr, E.M., Ng, R.T.: A unified notion of outliers: properties and computation. In: KDD, vol. 97, pp. 219–222 (1997)
13. Kohavi, R.: A study of cross-validation and bootstrap for accuracy estimation and model selection. In: International Joint Conference on Artificial Intelligence (1995)
14. Kuang, L., Zulkernine, M.: An anomaly intrusion detection method using the CSI-KNN algorithm. In: Proceedings of the 2008 ACM Symposium on Applied Computing, pp. 921–926 (2008)
15. Li, G., Tan, J., Chaudhry, S.S.: Industry 4.0 and big data innovations. Enterp. Inf. Syst. **13**(2), 145–147 (2019). https://doi.org/10.1080/17517575.2018.1554190
16. Lu, H., Guo, L., Azimi, M., Huang, K.: Oil and gas 4.0 era: a systematic review and outlook. Comput. Ind. **111**, 68–90 (2019)
17. Milojevic, S.: Sustainable application of natural gas as engine fuel in city buses: benefit and restrictions. Istrazivanja i Projektovanja za Privredu **15**(1), 81–88 (2017)
18. Naseer, S., Faizan Ali, R., Dominic, P., Saleem, Y.: Learning representations of network traffic using deep neural networks for network anomaly detection: a perspective towards oil and gas it infrastructures. Symmetry **12**(11), 1882 (2020)
19. Qiu, Z., Zhao, W., Hu, S., Zhang, G., Hui, F.: The natural gas resource potential and its important status in the coming low-carbon economy. Eng. Sci. **13**(6), 81–87 (2011)
20. Ramaswamy, S., Rastogi, R., Shim, K.: Efficient algorithms for mining outliers from large data sets. In: Proceedings of the 2000 ACM SIGMOD International Conference on Management of Data, pp. 427–438 (2000)
21. Shaikh, F., Ji, Q.: Forecasting natural gas demand in china: logistic modelling analysis. Int. J. Electr. Power Energy Syst. **77**, 25–32 (2016)
22. Vu, H.Q., Luo, J.M., Ye, B.H., Li, G., Law, R.: Evaluating museum visitor experiences based on user-generated travel photos. J. Travel Tourism Market. **35**(4), 493–506 (2018). https://doi.org/10.1080/10548408.2017.1363684
23. Xia, H., Vu, H.Q., Law, R., Li, G.: Evaluation of hotel brand competitiveness based on hotel features ratings. Int. J. Hospitality Manage. **86**, 102366 (2020). https://doi.org/10.1016/j.ijhm.2019.102366, https://www.sciencedirect.com/science/article/pii/S0278431919303019
24. Zhou, Z.H.: Ensemble Methods: Foundations and Algorithms. CRC Press, Boca Raton (2012)

A Framework Based Isolation Forest for Detecting Anomalies in Natural Gas Production

Shujuan Chen[1], Zhenjia Wang[2], Liping Liu[2], Yang Liu[2], Hu Chen[2], and Xichen Tang[3](✉)

[1] China Cybersecurity Review Technology and Certification Center, Beijing, China
chensj@isccc.gov.cn
[2] The First Gas Production Plant of Changqing Oilfield Branch, Xi'an, China
{wzj_cq,liulp001_cq,liuy03_cq,chenh1_cq}@petrochina.com.cn
[3] Qingdao University of Technology, Qingdao, China

Abstract. Natural gas is one of the main fossil fuels, and it is widely used in residential and industrial applications. The demand for natural gas is constantly increasing. However, due to the complex and diverse production environment for gas production, abnormal events that occur during the production of natural gas wells will reduce the gas production of gas wells with sufficient gas reservoirs. At present, detecting abnormal event in gas production mainly relies on engineers according to their own experience. This method is unreliable and requires a lot of manpower. In this paper, the first unsupervised framework for detecting anomalies in natural gas production is proposed. In this framework, a novel data convention method using a time window is proposed to enable the capture of the contextual anomaly. Besides, a low time-complexity and a small memory-requirement method called Isolation Forest is used to build a detector. Moreover, the maximum information coefficient (MIC) based feature selection mechanism reduces the high dimension caused by data convention in order to solve the increasing complexity of natural gas data sets. We apply our framework to several real natural gas well production data set labeled manually. Observations show that this framework increases the accuracy of the detection in the actual gas well production.

Keywords: Natural gas · Anomaly detection · Isolation forest

1 Introduction

Natural gas is a clean and cheap fossil fuel compared with other energy sources such as oil and coal. Industrial development and electricity generation are heavily dependent on the supply of natural gas [4]. It is also used as compressed natural gas (CNG) to provide fuel for millions of vehicles [12]. However, natural gas wells often have low productivity in practical gas production. The low gas production of such wells is not due to the small natural gas reserves, but is

S. R. Pokhrel et al. (Eds.): ATIS 2021, CCIS 1554, pp. 96–108, 2022.
https://doi.org/10.1007/978-981-19-1166-8_8

affected by various abnormal event such as fluid accumulation and blockage in the production process, so that the production capacity is suppressed.

Figure 1 shows a data recorded by three sensors during the practical production processing of natural gas wells. As show in Fig. 1, each sensor records the value of a related factor with time. Combined with those record, it can be seen that a large number of abnormal events exist in the actual production process. If these abnormal events cannot be detected and processed in time, it will cause a large number of production reductions or even machine losses, and waste a lot of manpower and material resources.

At present, detecting the abnormal event during gas wells production mainly relies on engineers according to their own experience, which requires engineers to continuously monitor the status of gas wells and take corresponding measures for different gas wells. However, this subjective method relying on engineers not only consumes a lot of manpower but also is inefficient. The detection accuracy of this method is not enough.

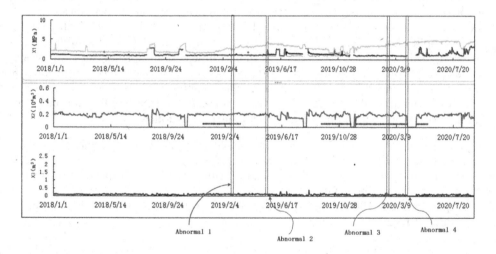

Fig. 1. Gas production curve of a gas well.

In the area of data mining and machine learning, many methods are proposed to automatic detect anomalies. It have been used for detecting any abnormal events such as intrusion detection [6], fault detection [8], and event detection in social networks [1,2]. However, as best as we know, there is no literature about detecting an abnormal event in gas well production using machine learning. This work aims to enhance the ability to detect abnormal events in gas production by introducing machine learning methods.

Many factors need to be considered in the judgment of abnormal production of natural gas wells.

1. The recorded data in gas well production are unlabeled. It is difficult to obtain labels of large amounts of data.

2. The detection of anomalies needs to consider multivariate. Only relying on a single feature is often unable to accurately judge.
3. The relationship between its contexts also needs to be considered in detecting anomalies. Events often appear to be normal at a specific time point, but when considering the context, it will be found that it is actually abnormal.
4. The anomaly detection of gas well production requires not only accurate detection of anomalies, but also rapid detection to adapt to the continuous data.

Those considerations make it become a very challenge to accurately detect anomalies in the process of natural gas well production.

To overcome those challenges, an unsupervised anomaly detection framework is proposed for gas well production, which will be used to quickly detect abnormal events in gas production. We convert the data to the form of context dependent using a time window method to capture the relationship between sample and its contextual information. Isolatin Forest is an anomaly detection algorithm which inspired by the potential difference between abnormalities data and abnormal data. Its working principle is to separate each sample in the data set and split them into abnormal data or normal data. Abnormal samples can be easily isolated since the number of them are less than normal data samples in dataset. Appropriate feature selection methods can reduce the computational burden of the model. Maximum Information Coefficien [3] is used for feature selection since it could detect more feature correlations than traditional ones.

The contributions of our work are summarized as follows:

- The framework based on unsupervised machine learning method is firstly proposed to detect anomalies in gas well production;
- A novel data covention method based on time window is proposed to detect the contextual abnormal.
- Experiments on the actual production data of several gas wells show that our proposed framework performs.

The rest of this paper is organized as follows: The principles of gas well and realted anomaly detection algorithms are described in Sect. 2. In the Sect. 3, the proposed anomly detection framework is detaily introduced step by step. Experimental settings and results are detailed in Sect. 4; Finally, the conclusion and future works are discussed in Sect. 5.

2   Related Work

At present, the abnormal detection of gas well production mainly relies on the engineer's experience to make manual judgments [13]. However, this method that completely depends on the engineer's experience often results in great differences in the results due to the engineer's subjective judgment, and the judgment results do not have the actual production guidance function. Machine Learning has been utilized in a great variety of areas such as social media [17,18], social science [19] and industrial [10,20]. With the continuous mining of anomaly detection value, it attracts the attention of researchers in Machine Learning. Researchers have proposed a variety of algorithms based on different perspectives and data. However, as best as we know, the research about detecting abnormal event in gas well production using machine learning method has not been reported.

The classical algorithms are roughly divided into parametric and nonparametric method. The parametric algorithm fits the overall distribution of the data according to the descriptive statistics of the data [16], such as the mean and variance. The values deviating from a certain threshold of the mean and variance are considered as outliers. However, the problem of this kind of algorithm is that the abnormal values are highly sensitive to these statistics [14], resulting in the fitting distribution deviating from the distribution of normal data, so that some values with small abnormal degrees are detected as normal.

The parameterized method assumes that the overall distribution is known (usually assumed to normal distribution). The idea is to use the distribution of the mean and variance to identify outliers. It works well when the overall data change is relatively stable. However, for the data with similar large fluctuations, the effect is unsatisfactory.

The common idea of non-parametric is to define outliers based on density, distance and establish Isolation forests to obtain outliers. Local Outlier Factor (LOF) [5] is classical density-based algorithm. The outlier recognition of this algorithm depends on the density-reachable definition. This algorithm has achieved great results, but sometimes it ignores the distance information, which may not be very effective for streamline data detection. In LOF, k nearest neighbor is based on Euclidean distance. This indirectly assumes that the distribution of data around the sample in a spherical manner. However, when processing the linear correlation data, this density estimation method is flawed.

The classical of the distance-based algorithm is KNN algorithm [15]. The nearest K points around the sample point are used to measure the anomaly degree between the sample points. This algorithm is much more advanced than the use of all data, but there may be a problem of ignoring local information. Whether it is based on the global KNN algorithm or the LOF algorithm, the output results are exceptionally abnormal score. However, the existing problem is the lack of a measurement standard to determine the abnormal value. The LoOP algorithm attempts to output probability values to overcome this problem [9], so that the data between different samples can better compare the degree of exception. To transform outliers into probabilities, this algorithm uses a normalization function and a Gaussian error function. Obviously, the probability of determining the outliers also has some subjectivity. With the development of machine learning, subsequent researchers used clustering algorithm for anomaly detection.

Isolation Forest was proposed by Liu et al. [11]. Different from the algorithm based on distance and density, it achieved the purpose of isolated outliers through the binary tree searching for sample points. The outliers are defined by comparing the path length of the sample points with the average path length of the binary tree. Compared with traditional algorithms such as statistic description and COF, the Isolation Forest algorithm has a good robustness at high dimension datasets.

3   Anomaly Detection Framework

The purpose of gas well abnormality detection is to judge the current status of the gas well based on historical multiple variables, which is: input is the set of observed feature vectors $\{X\}_{t=1}^{T} = \{x_1, x_2, \cdots, x_T\}$ where $x_t \in R^m$ and T is the length of the total time step, such as the number of days in the collected data set. The time step is t, $y_t \in \{0, 1\}$ is the production state of the sample. The gas well anomaly detection problem use multivariate $\{X\}_{t=1}^{T}$ as input to find a model f is constructed to judge the current gas well status y_t, namely:

$$\hat{y}_t = f\left(\{x_t\}_{t=1}^{T}\right) \tag{1}$$

Aiming at the characteristics of gas production data from gas wells, we establishe a gas well anomaly detection framework as shown in Fig. 2. The proposed framework is divided into two modules where the first one is the data preprocessing stage, including data conversion and feature extraction. The second one is the design and training of the anomaly detection model.

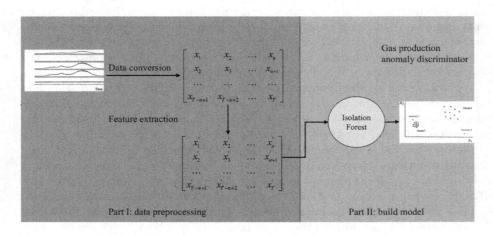

Fig. 2. Intelligent gas well anomaly detection framework.

3.1   Data Conversion

Gas well data is a kind of sequence data that changes over time. Let $\{X\}_{t=1}^{T} = \{x_1, x_2, \cdots, x_T\}$ represent T gas production data samples where $x_t \in R^m$. Let

n represent the lag input quantity where $n \in \{1, 2, \cdots, T-1\}$. If only using the current time data cannot capture the impact of historical data on the current decision, and cannot judge the current anomaly through context information. Therefore, it is necessary to transform the gas production data input with historical data.

In proposed framework, a time window which size is n is used to capture contextual information. The collected time series data $X = \{x_1, x_2, \cdots, x_T\}$ of gas production can be converted into the data form as shown in Eq. 2. The right matrix will be used as the input of the anomaly detection model ($\{v_1, v_2, \cdots, v_n\}$ represents n independent variables).

$$
\begin{pmatrix} x_1 \ x_2 \dots x_T \end{pmatrix} \rightarrow
\begin{pmatrix}
v_1 & v_2 & \dots & v_n \\
x_1 & x_2 & \dots & x_n \\
x_2 & x_3 & \dots & x_{n+1} \\
\dots & \dots & \dots & \dots \\
x_{T-n} & x_{T-n+1} & \dots & x_T
\end{pmatrix}
\tag{2}
$$

That is using the last n observation samples of gas production data to detecte the state of gas production at the current time.

3.2   Feature Extraction

Through the above-mentioned data conversion steps, the dimensionality of the input data is increased to $m \times n$, and the increase of the dimensionality is prone to dimensional disasters. A large amount of redundant information makes the model training difficult to converge and the training speed is reduced. We use the maximum information coefficient (MIC) [3] to filter the feature of high correlation so that the dimension is reduced to $m^{'} \times n^{'}$, where $m^{'} \times n^{'} < m \times n$. The retained features are maximized and remain independent of each other. Compared with the most commonly used Pearson correlation coefficient, MIC can overcome the limitation of maximum linearity and can find more relevant types of features.

We first briefly introduce the theory of mutual information as a prerequisite for understanding MIC. Let A and B indicates two random variables with discrete values. Mutual information is used to measure the decrease in uncertainty about the variable after observing anather variable, or measure the decrease in uncertainty after observing the variable through symmetry. It can be calculated by Eq. 3.

$$
I(A; B) = \sum_{a \in A} \sum_{b \in B} p(a, b) \log \frac{p(a, b)}{p(a)p(b)}
\tag{3}
$$

According to Eq. 3, if $I(A; B) = 0$ then the variables A and B are independent; Otherwise, A and B has correlation. In this case, the larger the value of Mutual information is, the higher correlation between two variables.

Given two variables A and B and a finite data set $D = \{a_i, b_i\}$, where $|D| = n$, assuming that the A, B axes are divided into n_a, n_b bins, respectively.

Let G represents obtained $n_a \times n_b$ grid. Then the probability distribution $D|_G$ can be approximatly calculated by the ratio of data points falling into grids.

Given a data set $D \in R^2$ and the grid $n_a \times n_b$, the maximum mutual information is defined as:

$$I^*(D, n_a, n_b) = \max I\left(D|_G\right) \tag{4}$$

where $I\left(D|_G\right)$ is the mutual information of the data set D under the gird G.

The elements of the characteristic matrix $M(D)$ of the data set D is defined as

$$M(D)_{n_a, n_b} = \frac{I^*(D, n_a, n_b)}{\log \min\{n_a, n_b\}} \tag{5}$$

where $\log \min\{n_a, n_b\}$ normalize all entities of the matrix $M(D)$ falls into the domain $[0, 1]$.

The MIC value of the data set $D(|D| = n)$ with two variables is defined as.

$$\text{MIC}(D) = \max_{n_a \times n_b \leq B(n)} \{M(D)_{n_a, n_b}\} \tag{6}$$

where default value $B(n) = n^{0.6}$.

3.3   Isolation Forest Algorithm

The Isolation Forest algorithm is designed using two features of the anomaly data: a. The proportion of abnormal data in the overall size of the dataset is small. b. There are significant differences in attribute values between abnormal samples and normal samples. The concept of iTrees, the path length and the anomaly score of Isolation Forest are explained as follows:

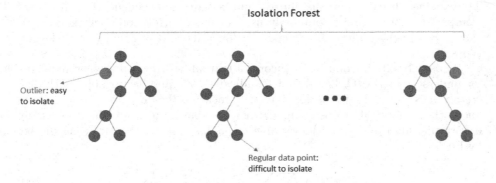

Fig. 3. Isolation forest

Isolation Tree. An Isolation Tree (iTree) is a complete binary tree, in which each internal node has two children and each leaf node has no child node. After separating each different sample into a leaf node, a binary tree as shown in Fig. 3

is given. Let $D = [d_1, d_2, \cdots, d_n]$ be the gas data set after MIC transformation, which is composed of n samples, and each sample is composed of r features. In order to construct iTree, we use D', $D' \subset D$, consisting of m samples, a feature x_j is randomly seltected from r features, and a split value p to perform a test i.e. whether $x_j < p$. The data samples are divided into two sub-tree T_l and T_r according this test. This process is recursively repeated until one of the following conditions is satisfied: only one sample in T_l and T_r or all samples at T_l and T_r have the same value. After build iTree using D, the number of leaf nodes in iTree is m, the number of internal nodes is $m - 1$, and the total number of nodes in iTree is $2\,m - 1$.

Path Length. Path length is a measure of isolation sensitivity in Isolation Forest algorithm. Given a sample x and an iTree, the number of edges passed from the root node to the leaf node which has x in the iTree is called the path length $h(x)$. In other words, in the recursive splitting process at tree level, the number of splittings required for separating samples is the path length from root node to leaf node. For a specific sample in a iTree, the following viewpoints are considered:

- The sample with long path length corresponds to low susceptibility to be isolated.
- The sample with short path length corresponds to high susceptibility to be isolated.

Anomaly Score. Anomaly score, as other anomaly detection methods, is used to make a decision on a sample in iTree. The maximum height of an iTree increases at $O(m)$, but its average height increases at $O(\log(m))$. Using m or $\log(m)$ to normalize the path length of different sub-sampling size models is not bounded, and it is impossible to directly compare the path length. Thus the average path length $c(m)$ of an iTree is estimated using a method in binary search trees which structure is the same as iTrees. Given the dataset m, the anomaly score S of a sample d_i is defined as follows:

$$S(m, d_i) = 2^{-\frac{-E(P(d_i))}{c(m)}} \tag{7}$$

where $P(d_i)$ is the path length of d_i in an iTree, $E(h(d))$ is the average of the path length over all iTrees, and $c(m)$ is the average path length of failed query in a binary search tree.

The relationships between $E(P(d_i))$ and the value of the anomaly score are given as follows:

- when $E(h(d)) \to C(n)$, $S \to 0.5$
- when $E(h(d)) \to 0$, $S \to 1$
- when $E(h(d)) \to n - 1$, $S \to 0$

For samples in dataset, if the vaules returned by the S are close to 1, they are regarded as anomalies; if the exception scores of samples are far less than 0.5, they are safely classified as normal; when all samples return 0.5 abnormal scores, the whole samples has no obvious or obvious exception.

3.4 Advantages of Isolation Forest

Applying Isolation Forest model in detecting anomalies in natural gas production has those major advantages:

- It is very difficult to obtain the label of abnormal production in gas well production. The Isolation Forest is a classical unsupervised anomaly detection algorithm.
- The isolation Forest model is based on the ensemble method, which provides better tools to improve the detection accuracy in gas well production.
- Isolated forest can use sub-sampling to achieve low time complexity and small memory requirements. These characteristics meet the needs of scalability and rapid detection of anomalies in a large number of gas well production data.

4   Experimental Results

4.1 Data Preparation

Due to device limitations and data availability, our datasets include six features as shown below:

- Working hour. Working hours of the day for a well.
- Tubing pressure. Tubing pressure is the residual pressure of oil and gas flowing from the bottom hole to the wellhead.
- Casing pressure. The pressure gauge for measuring casing pressure is connected with the annular space between the oil pipe and the casing. Its size reflects the annular space pressure and the amount of natural gas separated from the oil.
- Entrance pressure. Entrance pressure refers to the difference between the set pressure of the upstream station and the pressure loss in the midway.
- Daily gas production. Total daily gas production of gas wells.
- Daily water production. Total daily water production of gas wells.

The gas plant engineers have already manually labelled the anomalies for the four datasets. We have aligned all sensor features to the same timestamp over the available data collection periods. The original data characteristics of the 4 data sets are shown in Table 1. Each gas well has different anomaly rates and time series lengths.

4.2 Baseline

The coventional mehtod used in the natural gas industry are based on two rules, provided by the engineers from the gas factory.

1. The fluctuation of daily water production is a key condition to detect abnormal gas wells. If the daily water production in 3 days is higher than the n times average daily water production in the previous 10 days, it will consider the gas well abnormal. The value of n can be referred to Table 2.

Table 1. Description of gas well data.

Data set	Number of samples	Ratio of abnormalities	Data dimension
Gas well # 1	7406	0.07%	5
Gas well # 2	5306	4.41%	5
Gas well # 3	6339	5.68%	5
Gas well # 4	7403	10.44%	5

Table 2. Parameter value of daily water production

Daily water production(m^3/day)	Parameter n
[0,2)	2
(2,5]	1
(5,10]	0.8
(10,+∞]	0.5

2. If the casing pressure keeps rising during the working hours such that the average daily casing pressure is larger than that of the previous date, the gas well will be classified as abnormal.

We use these two rules together, i.e. if one of them is met, the gas well is judged as abnormal.

4.3   Paramter Setting

The experiment of Isolated Forest on real gas production data is divided into two stages: training the model and evaluating it. For each dataset, 80% of the dataset are used to train the model and the remaining 20% of the dataset as testing the trained model. The number of sampling samples ψ and the number of iTree t in the Isolation Forest model are the parameters that mainly affect the detection accuracy. Through parameter searching, the number of sampling samples $\psi = 128$ and the number of iTree $t = 200$ is selected since they can achieve the best detection accuracy.

4.4   Experimental Results

ROC is used indicator to measure the effectiveness of proposed framework. The ROC curve [7] summarizes the performance of the detection scheme on all possible thresholds. It is achieved by using confusion matrix to draw false positive rate (FPR) and true positive rate (TPR). The confusion matrix explains the performance of the test data set detection model where the true or actual values are known.

- FPR is the probability that normal samples are incorrectly identified by detector as being abnormal. It is used as a measure of the specificity of the abnormal detector.
- TPR is the probability that the abnormal samples are correctly identified by detector as the abnormal data.

The value of ROC close to 1 verifies the good performance of the method. In an anomaly detector, the detection result is related to the preset threshold (greater than the threshold is 1, less than the threshold is 0). If the threshold is set to be very small, then more and more abnormal samples will be correctly judged. Then the true positive rate naturally rises, but at the same time, more and more normal samples are incorrectly predicted as abnormal, so the false positive rate also rises.

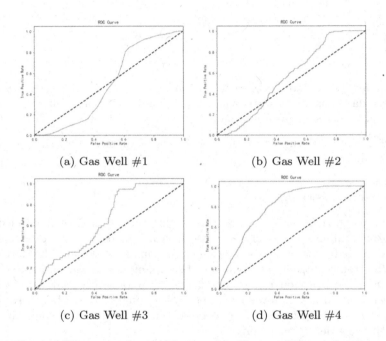

(a) Gas Well #1   (b) Gas Well #2

(c) Gas Well #3   (d) Gas Well #4

Fig. 4. AUC scores of ensemble tree algorithm on different datasets

The ROC curve of the proposed framework on the data set is shown in Fig. 4. It can be seen that for gas wells with different abnormal ratios, the proposed framework can detect anomalies. And with the increase of the proportion of abnormal data, the higher the accuracy of the detection.

Table 3 shows the ROC values performances of coventional method and iForest. It shows that iForest outperforms conventional methods on all datasets. It is worth noting that on the #1 gas well having small ratio of abnormalities, our proposed framwork still performs well.

Table 3. ROC values for different methods.

Methods	Gas well #1	Gas well #2	Gas well #3	Gas well #4
Conventional	0.54	0.54	0.53	0.51
IForest	0.58	0.60	0.69	0.81

5   Conclusion

Natural gas as a clean and cheap fossil fuel has been widly used in industrial and commercial sectors. Gas well abnormality judgment occupies an important position in actual gas production. In this paper, an unsupervised framework for detecting anomalies in natural gas production is proposed, taking into account the real scene of unlabeled historical data sets. In this framework, a novel data covention method using time window is proposed to enable the framework could capture the contextual anomaly. In order to solve the increasing complexity of natural gas data sets, the Maximum Information Coefficien-based feature selection mechanism is used to maximize the reduce the dataset from high-dimensional to low-dimensional. Moreover, a low time-complexity and a small memory-requirement anomaly detection method called Isolated Forest is firstly used in detect the abnormal event in gas well production. The proposed framework has low computational complexity and can identify anomalies in a short time. We apply our framework to real natural gas well production data labeled manually. The results of experience show that our detection framework credibly improves the detection accuracy in the actual gas well production.

As a future research direction, more diversified features will be collected and considered to enhance the framework, and we will combine more abnormal detection algorithms to improve the accuracy and speed of detection in gas well production.

References

1. Alallaq, N., Al-khiza'ay, M., Dohan, M.I., Han, X.: Sentiment analysis to enhance detection of latent astroturfing groups in online social networks. In: Chen, Q., Wu, J., Zhang, S., Yuan, C., Batten, L., Li, G. (eds.) ATIS 2018. CCIS, vol. 950, pp. 79–91. Springer, Singapore (2018). https://doi.org/10.1007/978-981-13-2907-4_7
2. Alallaq, N., Al-khiza'ay, M., Han, X.: Group topic-author model for efficient discovery of latent social astroturfing groups in tourism domain. Cybersecurity **2**(1), 1–11 (2019). https://doi.org/10.1186/s42400-019-0029-8
3. Albanese, D., Riccadonna, S., Donati, C., Franceschi, P.: A practical tool for maximal information coefficient analysis. Oxford Open **7**(4), giy032 (2018)
4. Lin, B., Wesseh, P.K., Jr.: Estimates of inter-fuel substitution possibilities in Chinese chemical industry. Energy Econ. **40**(2), 560–568 (2013)
5. Breunig, M.M., Kriegel, H.P., Ng, R.T., Sander, J.: Lof: identifying density-based local outliers. In: Proceedings of the 2000 ACM SIGMOD International Conference on Management of Data, pp. 93–104 (2000)

6. Garcia-Teodoro, P., Diaz-Verdejo, J., Maciá-Fernández, G., Vázquez, E.: Anomaly-based network intrusion detection: techniques, systems and challenges. Comput. Secur. **28**(1–2), 18–28 (2009)
7. Hanley, J.A., Mcneil, B.J.: The meaning and use of the area under a receiver operating characteristic (roc) curve. Radiology **143**(1), 29 (1982)
8. Hwang, I., Kim, S., Kim, Y., Seah, C.E.: A survey of fault detection, isolation, and reconfiguration methods. IEEE Trans. Control Syst. Technol. **18**(3), 636–653 (2009)
9. Kriegel, H.P., Kröger, P., Schubert, E., Zimek, A.: Loop: local outlier probabilities. In: Proceedings of the 18th ACM Conference on Information and Knowledge Management, pp. 1649–1652 (2009)
10. Li, G., Tan, J., Chaudhry, S.S.: Industry 4.0 and big data innovations. Enterp. Inf. Syst. **13**(2), 145–147 (2019). https://doi.org/10.1080/17517575.2018.1554190
11. Liu, F.T., Ting, K.M., Zhou, Z.H.: Isolation forest. In: 2008 Eighth IEEE International Conference on Data Mining, pp. 413–422. IEEE (2008)
12. Milojevic, S.: Sustainable application of natural gas as engine fuel in city buses: benefit and restrictions. Istrazivanja i Projektovanja za Privredu **15**(1), 81–88 (2017)
13. Naseer, S., Faizan Ali, R., Dominic, P., Saleem, Y.: Learning representations of network traffic using deep neural networks for network anomaly detection: a perspective towards oil and gas it infrastructures. Symmetry **12**(11), 1882 (2020)
14. Ord, K.: Outliers in statistical data. In: Barnett, V., Lewis, T. (eds.) 3rd edition, Wiley, Chichester, 584 p. [UK pound]55.00, 175–176 (1994), ISBN 0-471-93094-6. Int. J. Forecast. **12**(1) (1996). https://ideas.repec.org/a/eee/intfor/v12y1996i1p175-176.html
15. Ramaswamy, S., Rastogi, R., Shim, K.: Efficient algorithms for mining outliers from large data sets. In: Proceedings of the 2000 ACM SIGMOD International Conference on Management of Data, pp. 427–438 (2000)
16. Rousseeuw, P.J., Hubert, M.: Robust statistics for outlier detection. Wiley Interdisc. Rev. Data Min. Knowl. Discovery **1**(1), 73–79 (2011)
17. Subramani, S., Wang, H., Vu, H.Q., Li, G.: Domestic violence crisis identification from Facebook posts based on deep learning. IEEE Access **6**, 54075–54085 (2018). https://doi.org/10.1109/ACCESS.2018.2871446
18. Vu, H.Q., Luo, J.M., Ye, B.H., Li, G., Law, R.: Evaluating museum visitor experiences based on user-generated travel photos. J. Travel Tourism Market. **35**(4), 493–506 (2018). https://doi.org/10.1080/10548408.2017.1363684
19. Xia, H., Vu, H.Q., Law, R., Li, G.: Evaluation of hotel brand competitiveness based on hotel features ratings. Int. J. Hospitality Manage. **86**, 102366 (2020). https://doi.org/10.1016/j.ijhm.2019.102366, https://www.sciencedirect.com/science/article/pii/S0278431919303019
20. Zhu, T., Li, G., Zhou, W., Xiong, P., Yuan, C.: Privacy-preserving topic model for tagging recommender systems. Knowl. Inf. Syst. **46**(1), 33–58 (2015). https://doi.org/10.1007/s10115-015-0832-9

A Survey of BGP Anomaly Detection Using Machine Learning Techniques

Noor Hadi Hammood[1]([envelope]), Bahaa Al-Musawi[2], and Ahmed Hazim Alhilali[3]

[1] Department of Computer Science Faculty of Computer Science and Mathematics,
University of Kufa, An Najaf, Iraq
noorh.hammood@student.uokufa.edu.iq
[2] Department of Electronics and Communication Engineering Faculty of Engineering,
University of Kufa, An Najaf, Iraq
[3] Information Technology Research and Development Centre,
University of Kufa, An Najaf, Iraq

Abstract. The border gateway protocol (BGP) is the protocol underlying the Internet's global routing system. It manages the connectivity among autonomous systems (ASes) and how the packets get routed from one network to another. This survey focused on extracting all the possible BGP features from a BGP control plane and determining the most significant ones for detecting BGP abnormalities. Also, it provides a review of the recent works concerned with using Machine Learning algorithms to detect BGP anomalies.

Keywords: BGP · BGP features · Machine learning · Anomaly detection

1 Introduction

Border Gateway Protocol (BGP) is an exterior gateway protocol. It is a route vector protocol that manages Network Reachability Information (NRI) between Autonomous Systems (ASes). An AS is a group of routers that work together under a single technical, administrative authority. Each AS has a unique identifier called an AS number for each AS in the public or private AS number space [1]. BGP establishes a reliable connection on the Transport Control Protocol (TCP) at port 179. Classless Inter-Domain Routing (CIDR) is supported by a set of mechanisms that BGP implements to provide Internet Protocol (IP) addressing hierarchical architecture, AS route aggregation, incremental enhancements, and routing policies setting ability well as improve the filtering options [2]. The purpose of BGP is to help an organization achieve its business goals by providing NRI to other organizations [3].

Anomalies in BGP represent any BGP behavior that does not contribute to or hinder those business objectives. Unfortunately, determining whether or not a certain action is achieving those aims may be difficult. For example, BGP updates that do not match underlying topology changes may or may not be anomalies. They might be the consequence of real policy changes or route flapping, which occurs when routes are frequently advertised and then swiftly retracted [4]. Unusual occurrences such as power outages

© Springer Nature Singapore Pte Ltd. 2022
S. R. Pokhrel et al. (Eds.): ATIS 2021, CCIS 1554, pp. 109–120, 2022.
https://doi.org/10.1007/978-981-19-1166-8_9

and BGP misconfiguration by the network operator (also known as routing table leaks) can negatively affect the global routing stability and might interrupt Internet services for hours [3]. The following are some examples of anomaly events that impacted BGP routing efficiency;

The Turkish Telecom (TTNet) announced more than 100,000K incorrect routes on December 24, 2004. Another example, on 4 October 2021 around 15:40 UTC, AS32934 (Facebook outage) began withdrawal prefixes, On June 12, 2015, Telecom Malaysia (TMNet) BGP misconfiguration. AS 27506 hijacked the panix domain on January 14, 2005. The Moscow blackout link failure occurred on May 7, 2005. Dodo, an Australian company, caused a route leak incident on February 23, 2012, announcing all its internal routes to Telstra. Brazilian on July 21, 2020, AS 264462 announced more than 13046 prefixes in a networking event starting at 9.15 UTC and ending at 10.38, which continue for 1 h and 23 min [5]. The Indian network Vodafone's autonomous (AS55410) on April 16, 2021, announced more than 30,000 prefixes in a networking incident that started at 13:50 and ending 14:00 UTC [6]. And Slammer, Nimda, and Code Red I are examples of worm attacks. These examples demonstrate the need for an effective BGP anomaly detection system.

Several approaches that can improve BGP security rely on cryptographic authentication or anomaly detection; Cryptographic protocols consist of the Resource Public Key Infrastructure (RPKI) [7]. RPKI is a global authorization infrastructure used by network operators such as ISPs to confirm BGP route origination assertions. For example, the owner of a block of IP address version 4 or 6 can permit an AS to originate routes for that block by providing a Route Origination Authorization (ROA) [8]. RPKI helped to restrict Internet routing events such as hijacking and route leaks [9]. Unfortunately, RPKI has not shown its ability to prevent or mitigate BGP misconfiguration.

Internetworks have been endangered because of these consequences. A statistic by Xiang et al. [10] shows that events such as hijackings and misconfigurations can pollute 90% of the Internet in less than 2 min. Also, it shows that finding out more significant features could improve the detection process of different types of BGP anomalies. The network operators need to identify the anomaly type and take the necessary action where the procedure required to solve the link failure is different from the routing leak ones.

Today, Machine Learning (ML) approaches have enhanced BGP anomaly detection by using different types of BGP features, which are usually noisy and bursty [11]. Therefore, we will review some previous work in machine learning to detect the anomaly.

In this paper, we provide the fundamental operation of BGP and explore different types of BGP messages. We also explore all possible BGP features that have been used by previous works which can help to improve detection accuracy. Finally, we review the most significant works based on using machine learning techniques to detect BGP anomalies during the last five years.

2 BGP Background

BGP send incremental updates when the network's reachability or topology changes [1]. Announcements about new prefixes or withdrawals of existing prefixes are exchanged after that. All BGP messages contain the same header, which includes marker, length and type. Four main types of messages are sent and received by BGP routers (OPEN, UPDATE, KEEPALIVE, and NOTIFICATION) [3]. The BGP peers send OPEN message shortly after the TCP connection is established. It's used to start a BGP peering session by requesting one over an existing TCP connection and sending information to the BGP neighbor about the BGP node beginning the session. The BGP peers can exchange routing information through the UPDATE message. The information is used to generate a relationships graph between the different AS.

KEEPALIVE message sent between peers to ensure that the connection is still active during periods of inactivity. NOTIFICATION message used to notify about terminated BGP session when something is wrong with that session. A dedicated connection or Internet exchange point is used to exchange BGP routing information between ISPs in different geographical areas. The Routing Information Base (RIB) is a distributed database that keeps track of peer-to-peer routing connections.

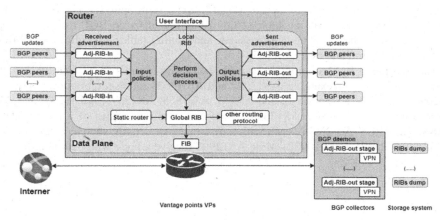

Fig. 1. BGP router architecture.

Each router has its own RIB, which stores routing information specific to that router. The best routes from all routing protocols functioning on the system are saved in a RIB, which is made up of three parts: Adj-RIB-In, Adj-RIB-Out, and Loc-RIB. The Adj-RIB-In refers to a set of input databases containing routing information delivered by peer BGP speakers to the local router. Their contents are routes that may be used as input to the path Decision Process.

The Loc-RIB comprises routing information that the local router chose after applying policy to the Adj-RIB-In routing information. These are the routes that the local router will utilize. The Adj-RIB-Out represents the core of RIB, and it stores the information that the local router has selected to broadcast to its peers. When this router advertises to peers, it sends out UPDATE messages that contain this information. In summary, the Adj-RIB-In includes unprocessed peer-to-peer routing information, the Loc-RIB has routes selected by the local BGP speaker's best-path decision procedure, and the Adj-RIB-Out contains routes for advertisement to peers in UPDATE messages. This architecture is depicted (see Fig. 1).

Each router sends an update message to its neighbor when the Adj-RIB-out changes, signaling that the Loc-RIB has changed. The collector dumps a snapshot of the Adj-RIB-Out tables as well as any update messages received since the last dump on a regular basis. These dumps provide you with detailed insight into the routing dynamics [1]. The RouteViews project and the RIPE NCC are two of the most prominent initiatives that provide useful information for networking research.

The RIPE routing information service (RIS) is a service offered by RIPE Networks. In 2001, the RIPE NCC started collecting and storing Internet routing data from multiple ASes throughout the globe via the RIS project [12]. BGP update messages were gathered every 15 min until July 23, 2003, and every 5 min after that, with BGP routing tables being updated every 8 h. RIS now has 25 Remote Route Collectors (RRCs) located all over the world [13].

RouteViews is a University of Oregon initiative that gathers BGP routing information from many backbone routers and distributes it across geographic borders [14]. The publicly available BGP update message was utilized for route analysis. The RouteViews project assembles BGP routing tables from a number of Cisco BGP routers located throughout the globe. BGP update messages and routing tables are collected in MRT format every 15 min and every 2 h [15].

An example of BGP topology for sample data taken from RIPE NCC at RCC05 on MAY 25, 2005. In this example, AS12922 and AS 13634 represent monitoring points, AS20932 represent a source AS, and AS513, AS 1853, AS25091, AS 13237, and AS 2497are intermediate ASes. AS13634 can receive multiple copies of a BGP update MESSAGES from AS 20932, each with a different path length, such as (1853 13237 20932) and (25091 2497 20932) while AS12992 receive a copy with path length (513 20932) [4] (see Fig. 2).

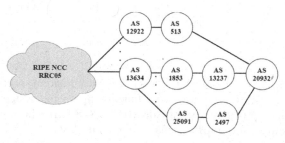

Fig. 2. BGP topology [4].

BGP raw data comes in three forms: control plane, data plane, and extra sources. The data for the control plane might be found in two well-known public sources (RouteViews project and RIPE NCC). The data plane is the mechanism through which BGP routes packets along the specified paths. Other sources of BGP data include bogon prefixes, RPKI data, and network operation mailing groups [3].

This survey focused on a BGP control plane data set to extract all possible BGP features and then determine which ones are most significant for detecting BGP abnormalities.

3 BGP Features

Different types of BGP features may obtained by extracting valuable information from the BGP control plane. AS-PATH and BGP volume (announcement/withdrawal) seem to be the most common two types of features. The total amount of BGP updates messages, including announcements and withdrawals, issued from an AS or a prefix during a period of time is referred to as BGP volume. The protocol may pick the optimum route to reach the packet's destination using a BGP update message with the AS-path property.

Encapsulated NLRI prefixes with identical BGP properties are transmitted in a single BGP packet. As a consequence, a BGP packet may include several NLRI prefixes that have been announced or withdrawn. AS-path lengths are calculated using the average and maximum number of AS peers. Table 1 shows the 55 BGP features specific to BGP updates messages and AS-Path length that were extracted [16]. The BGP features can mainly classified in to two types: Table 1 and Table 2 list the feature extracted from BGP volume and AS-path.

Table 1. The extracted BGP volume features.

ID	Feature	Description
1	BGP volume	Total number of BGP updates message (announcements and withdrawals)
2	No. announcements per prefix	The total number of announcements sent by the same prefix
3	No. withdrawals per prefix	The total number of withdrawals sent by the same prefix
4	No. duplicate announcements	BGP announcement with the same attributes
5	No. duplicate withdrawals	BGP withdrawals with the same attributes
6	No. new announcements	Re-announcement with at least one distinct attribute
7	No. IGP in the Origin attribute	Volume
8	No. EGP in the Origin attribute	Volume
9	No. INCOMPLETE in the Origin attribute	Volume
10	No. flaps	Re-announced path with the same BGP attribute
11	No. NADA	New announcement after withdrawal with different attributes
12	No. IPV4 announcements	Total number of IPV4 announcements per prefix
13	No. IPV4 withdrawals	Total number of IPV4 withdrawals per prefix
14	No. IPV6 announcements	Total number of IPV6 announcements per prefix

(continued)

Table 1. (*continued*)

ID	Feature	Description
15	No. IPV6 withdrawals	Total number of IPV6 withdrawals per prefix
16	NLRI	Total number of Network Layer Reachability Information per prefixes
17	NLRI announcements	Total number of Network Layer Reachability Information per announced prefixes
18	NLRI withdrawals	Total number of Network Layer Reachability Information per withdrawal prefixes
19	Inter arrival time	Volume
20	Packet size	Volume
21	Concentration ratio n = 1...3	Volume

Table 2. The extracted AS-path features.

ID	Feature	Description
1	Max AS-PATH length	The maximum length of AS-PATHs of all BGP update messages
2	Avg AS-PATH length	The average length of AS-PATHs of all BGP update messages
3	Max unique AS-PATH length	The max unique length of AS-PATHs of all BGP update messages
4	Avg unique AS-PATH length	The average unique length of AS-PATHs of all BGP update messages
5	Announcement to the shorter path	Announcement to the shorter AS-Path length
6	Announcement to the longer path	Announcement to the longer AS-Path length
7	Number of rare ASes	AS rarely appears in the BGP update messages
8	Max Number of rare ASes	The most rare AS appears in the BGP update messages
9	Avg of rare ASes	The average rare AS appears in the BGP update messages
10	Origin change	Re-announcement with new origin attributes

(*continued*)

Table 2. (*continued*)

ID	Feature	Description
11	Edit distance	The smallest number of (insertions, deletions, and substitutions) required to switch from one AS-path to another
12	Edit distance unique	The unique number of (insertions, deletions, and substitutions) required to switch from one AS-path to another [16]
13	max Edit distance	The maximum number of (insertions, deletions, and substitutions) required to switch from one AS-path to another [16]
14	Avg Edit distance	The average number of (insertions, deletions, and substitutions) required to switch from one AS-path to another [16]
15	Implicit withdrawal	The announcements for the same prefix in a row
16	Implicit withdrawal DPATH	Implicit withdrawal with the alternate path
17	Implicit withdrawal SPATH	Implicit withdrawal with the same path
18–27	Edit distance with k value where n = 1...10	Edit distance with specific k distance from the previous known path [16]
28–37	Edit distance unique with k value where n = 1...10	Edit distance with specific k distance from the previous known path for unique ASes [16]

4   Review of BGP Anomaly Detection Based on Machine Learning

Anomaly detection techniques are becoming increasingly prominent in the data mining sector because they recognize data items out of the ordinary for a given dataset. In big data management and data science, many anomaly detection techniques such as machine learning, time series, neural network techniques, supervised and unsupervised play a critical role in detecting fraud or other abnormal events.

In the recent years, several researchers try to develop BGP anomaly detection. In this section, we review the most significant and recent works during the last five years to detect BGP anomalies by using Machine learning algorithms.

Cheng Min et al. designed a unique Multi-Scale Long Short-Term Memory (MS-LSTM) mode for BGP anomaly detection. To gather temporal information on many scales, the MSLSTM employs a Discrete Wavelet Transform. They created a two-layer hierarchical LSTM architecture, with the first layer learning the attentions of various time scales and generating an integrated historical representation. The learnt representation was employed in the second layer to capture the time dependence. The authors used 33 features extracted from BGP update messages. They discovered that preprocessing the traffic flow on a different time scale had a substantial impact on the performance of all classifiers. Changing the time scale may enhance the accuracy of LSTM and other machine learning algorithms by roughly 10%, according to the research. In the best-case scenario, MS-LSTM with ideal time scale eight can achieve 99.5% accuracy [17].

Cosovic et al. proposed an approach to detect the BGP anomaly that depended on Artificial Neural Network (ANN) models with two hidden layers based on a back propagation algorithm. During the BGP events of the routing leak, worm, and power outage, the authors exploited BGP update messages to extract 15 features. All these events caused large-scale Internet outages. They discovered that BGP volume and AS-PATH information collected from BGP update messages might be used to accurately classify abnormal events. The high classification accuracy is obtained when using oversampling algorithms. However, in this approach, only 15 features have been used. A high accuracy detection process is required to extract all possible features and find the most relevant features [18].

Hashem et al. proposed an approach consisting of two stages: in the first stage, a Guide Feature Generator (GFG) algorithm is used to extract two types of features from BGP update messages, which are the traditional ones (16) and the guide features (16). The outcome of the first stage is used in the second stage, where it is forwarded to the proposed algorithm to automatically obtain the most dominant features (ASMDF) to reduce processing time and computations. Experimental evaluations performance was done by using multiple Machine learning techniques. Furthermore, when compared to previous methods, the suggested methodology speeds up and improves the process of identifying indirect anomalies by three times. The best accuracy rate was obtained is with RF is 0.9747 [19]. However, the suggested algorithms have not been tested with various forms of BGP traffic. It is possible to test the framework on different types of anomalies to verify the accuracy of the work on different types of anomalies. Furthermore, more features can be extracted from BGP update messages.

Dai Xianbo et al. proposed a support vector machine-based BGP anomaly detection technique (SVM-BGPAD) to address the issue of BGP anomalies. In this approach, 37 features have been extracted from BGP update messages. To choose the most important features, the authors employed a feature selection technique based on Fisher linear analysis and Markov random field technology. They evaluate the results by using SVM, a classification model. The RBF kernel function-based model has the highest classification accuracy of 91.36% and the highest F1-Score of 95.03% [20].

Li et al. suggested an anomaly detection technique based on recurrent neural networks (RNNs) to identify BGP abnormalities caused by the Slammer virus, WannaCrypt ransomware, and the Moscow blackout. They extracted 37 features during a one-minute time period using BGP update messages acquired from free sources such as RouteViews and RIPE NCC. As a consequence, when utilizing RouteViews datasets instead of RIPE NCC datasets, RNN classification models had a higher accuracy with LSTM model. However, the method has not been tested with other kinds of BGP anomalies [21].

Sanchez et al. identified a number of graph features for detecting BGP abnormalities. The BGP update message was collected via public monitoring services such the RIPE Routing Information Service (RIS) at RRC04 (Geneva) and RRC05 (Vienna). Authors extract 14 features every five minutes to detect BGP path leaks. They also compare several machine learning methods, such as Naive Bayes (NB), Decision Trees (DT), Random

Forests (RF), SVM, and Multi-Layer Perceptron (MLP), to examine the features. As a consequence, the article demonstrates that SVM has a significant accuracy-to-recall trade-off. The graph features, on the other hand, are computationally expensive and cannot be employed in real-time [11].

Hoarau Kevin et al. presented BGP Machine Learning (BML), a tool for creating BGP datasets that collects bulk of the available features from the literature and the internet topology and allows the user to customize those features. They extracted 32 synthetic features and 14 BGP graph features from the BGP anomaly datasets. The author illustrates how BML may be used to provide a sufficient understanding of the BGP. They demonstrate BML's capability on the BGP anomaly caused by the 2017 Google leak. Principal component analysis revealed that machine learning technologies are effective to detecting BGP anomaly. However, the proposed method has not been tested on several types of BGP events. Also, the distinction between two different types of anomalies has not been verified through graphing and features extraction process for two similar and different events to distinguish the influencing features for each event [22].

Allahdadi et al. proposed a framework design that used machine learning algorithms to detect BGP anomalies. It used BGP update message data to extract 18 features during Internet worms' anomaly, including Nimda, Slammer, and CodeRed, as well as link failures anomaly such as the East Coast, Florida, and Hurricane Katrina. These features were used to differentiate between anomalies and regular BGP update messages and improve classification results. The SVM algorithm achieve accuracy 98% [23]. However, improving the outcomes needs to minimize false-positive rates while maintaining a high degree of detection precision. The framework did not have been tested with other types of BGP anomaly. Moreover, it was possible to test the data using more than one algorithm to verify the accuracy of the results.

The authors could be improved the proposed approach by using more features and testing with different types of anomalies. Table 3 shows a summary of above related works.

Table 3. Summary of literature review

Authors	Year	BGP features	ML algorithms	Tested with	Best accuracy
Cheng Min et al.	2016	Extracted 33 features	(multi-scale, LSTM, SVM, NB, AdaptBoost)	DDoS attacks	MS-LSTM = 99.5%
Cosovic et al.	2018	Extracted 15 features	- ANN	(RTL, DDoS attacks, power outage)	High classification accuracy is obtained when using oversampling algorithms

(continued)

Table 3. (*continued*)

Authors	Year	BGP features	ML algorithms	Tested with	Best accuracy
Hashem et al.	2019	Using Guide feature generator (GFG) algorithm to extracted traditional (16) and guide features (16) every minute	(CART, CIT, RF, GBM, ELM, SGD, SVM, BN)	DDoS attacks	RF with GFG = 0.9747
Dai Xianbo et al.	2019	Extracted 37 features	- SVM	DDoS attacks	SVM accuracy = 91.36% SVM F1-Score = 95.03%
Li et al.	2020	Extracted 37 features	- LSTM-GRU	(DDoS attacks, WannaCrypt, power outage)	LSTM (F1_score) RIPE = 75.20 Route Views = 81.77
Sanchez et al.	2020	Extracted 14 features every five minutes	(NB, DT, SVM, MLP)	(RTL)	SVM = 0.94
Hoarau Kevin et al.	2020	Used BML to extracting 32 synthetic features and 14 BGP's graphs features	- PCA	Google leak	PCA that showed that ML tools with many features might be promising, emphasizing the necessity to produce a large number of features
Allahdadi et al.	2021	Extracted 18 features	- SVM	(DDoS attacks, power outage)	SVM = 98%

5　Conclusion

This paper discussed eight significant works related to BGP anomaly detection by using different ML algorithms during the last five years. We examine these works from three factors: the first is extracting all the possible BGP features from a BGP control plane and determining the most significant ones for BGP anomaly detections. The second is machine learning approaches that have been employed to identify BGP abnormalities, including supervised, unsupervised techniques. The third is that the proposed detection models used machine learning based on the classifiers to evaluate the performance of extraction features by testing different types of events. Finally, we list the accuracy of each work during the testing process.

However, none of these significant researches use the retrieved BGP features to discriminate between all forms of abnormalities. To take the appropriate action, network operators must first determine the type of anomaly. For example, the technique needed for resolving a link failure differs from that for resolving a routing leak.

References

1. Rekhter, Y., Lis, T.: A Border Gateway Protocol 4 (BGP-4) (1994). https://tools.ietf.org/html/rfc1654. Accessed 20 Mar 2021
2. Fonseca, P., Mota, E.S., Bennesby, R., Passito, A.: BGP dataset generation and feature extraction for anomaly detection. In: Proceedings of the International Symposium on Computers and Communications, June 2019 (2019). https://doi.org/10.1109/ISCC47284.2019.8969619
3. Al-Musawi, B., Branch, P., Armitage, G.: BGP anomaly detection techniques: a survey. IEEE Commun. Surv. Tut. **19**(1), 377–396 (2017). https://doi.org/10.1109/COMST.2016.2622240
4. Fuller, V., Li, T.: Classless inter-domain routing (CIDR): the Internet address assignment and aggregation plan (2006)
5. Bush, R.: The resource public key infrastructure (RPKI) to router protocol. J. Chem. Inf. Model. (2013). https://tools.ietf.org/html/rfc6810
6. Lepinski, M., Kent, S., Kong, D.: A profile for route origin authorizations (ROAs). IETF, RFC, vol. 6482 (2012)
7. Murphy, S.: BGP security vulnerabilities analysis (2006). https://tools.ietf.org/html/rfc4272. Accessed 30 Mar 2021
8. Shi, X., Xiang, Y., Wang, Z., Yin, X., Wu, J.: Detecting prefix hijackings in the internet with argus. In: Proceedings of the 2012 Internet Measurement Conference, pp. 15–28 (2012)
9. Siddiqui, A.: Big route leak shows need for routing security, 22 July 2020. https://www.manrs.org/2020/07/big-route-leak-shows-need-for-routing-security/. Accessed 10 Aug 2021
10. Sharma, A.: Major BGP leak disrupts thousands of networks globally. https://www.bleepingcomputer.com/news/security/major-bgp-leak-disrupts-thousands-of-networks-globally/. Accessed 10 Aug 2021
11. Sanchez, O.R., Ferlin, S., Pelsser, C., Bush, R.: Comparing machine learning algorithms for BGP anomaly detection using graph features. In: Big-DAMA 2019 - Proceedings of the 3rd ACM CoNEXT Workshop on Big DAta, Machine Learning and Artificial Intelligence for Data Communication Networks, Part of CoNEXT 2019, pp. 35–41 (2019). https://doi.org/10.1145/3359992.3366640
12. Edwards, P., Cheng, L., Kadam, G.: Border gateway protocol anomaly detection using machine learning techniques. SMU Data Sci. Rev. **2**(1), 5 (2019)
13. Zhang, K.: Instability, security and anomaly detection in Border Gateway Protocol. University of California, Davis (2007)
14. Qi, Z.: AS Path-Prepending in the Internet and Its Impact on Routing-Decisions. Institute of Network Architecture Technical University of Munich (2006)
15. McPherson, D., Gill, V., Walton, D., Retana, A.: Border gateway protocol (BGP) persistent route oscillation condition (2002)

16. Graham, J.S.: BGP Tutorial
17. Hawkinson, J., Bates, T.: Guidelines for creation, selection, and registration of an Autonomous System (AS). RFC 1930 (March 1996)
18. Caesar, M., Rexford, J.: BGP routing policies in ISP networks. IEEE Netw. **19**(6), 5–11 (2005)
19. Gao, L.: On inferring autonomous system relationships in the Internet. IEEE/ACM Trans. Netw. **9**(6), 733–745 (2001)
20. Hashem, M., Bashandy, A., Shaheen, S.: Improving anomaly detection in BGP time-series data by new guide features and moderated feature selection algorithm. Turk. J. Electr. Eng. Comput. Sci. **27**(1), 392–406 (2019). https://doi.org/10.3906/elk-1804-55
21. Moriano, P., Hill, R., Camp, L.J.: Using bursty announcements for detecting BGP routing anomalies. Comput. Netw. **188**, 107835 (2021)
22. University of Oregon: University of Oregon Route Views Project
23. Boaden, E.E.: Multi-threaded routing toolkit (MRT) border gateway protocol (BGP) routing information export format with geo-location extensions (2011). https://tools.ietf.org/html/rfc 6397
24. Al-Musawi, B., Branch, P., Armitage, G.: Detecting BGP instability using recurrence quantification analysis (RQA). In: 2015 IEEE 34th International Performance Computing and Communications Conference (IPCCC), pp. 1–8 (2015)
25. Hammood, N.H., Al-Musawi, B.: Using BGP features towards identifying type of BGP anomaly. In: 2021 International Congress of Advanced Technology and Engineering (ICOTEN), pp. 1–10 (2021)
26. Yujian, L., Bo, L.: A normalized Levenshtein distance metric. IEEE Trans. Pattern Anal. Mach. Intell. **29**(6), 1091–1095 (2007)
27. Blazakis, D., Baras, J.S.: Analyzing BGP ASPATH Behavior in the Internet. Syst. Res., no. January 2006 (2003)
28. de Urbina Cazenave, I.O., Köşlük, E., Ganiz, M.C.: An anomaly detection framework for BGP. In: 2011 International Symposium on Innovations in Intelligent Systems and Applications, pp. 107–111 (2011)
29. Al-rousan, N.M., Trajkovi, L.: Machine learning models for classification of BGP anomalies, pp. 103–108 (2012)
30. Cheng, M., Li, Q., Lv, J., Liu, W., Wang, J.: Multi-scale LSTM model for BGP anomaly classification. IEEE Trans. Serv. Comput. **14**, 765–778 (2018)
31. Cosovic, M., Obradovic, S., Junuz, E.: Deep learning for detection of BGP anomalies. In: Rojas, I., Pomares, H., Valenzuela, O. (eds.) ITISE 2017. CS, pp. 95–113. Springer, Cham (2018). https://doi.org/10.1007/978-3-319-96944-2_7
32. Dai, X., Wang, N., Wang, W.: Application of machine learning in BGP anomaly detection. J. Phys. Conf. Ser. **1176**(3), 32015 (2019)
33. Li, Z., Rios, A.L.G., Trajkovic, L.: Detecting internet worms, ransomware, and blackouts using recurrent neural networks. In: 2020 IEEE International Conference on Systems, Man, and Cybernetics, October 2020, pp. 2165–2172 (2020). https://doi.org/10.1109/SMC42975. 2020.9283472
34. Hoarau, K., Tournoux, P., Razafindralambo, T., An, B.M.L., Tool, V.: BML: an efficient and versatile tool for BGP dataset collection (2021). HAL Id: hal-03225786
35. Allahdadi, A., Morla, R., Prior, R.: A framework for BGP abnormal events detection. arXiv (2017)

Flow-Based Intrusion Detection Systems: A Survey

Aliaa Al-Bakaa$^{(\boxtimes)}$ and Bahaa Al-Musawi$^{(\boxtimes)}$

Faculty of Engineering, University of Kufa, Najaf, Iraq
aliaam.albakaa@student.uokufa.edu.iq,
bahaa.almusawi@uokufa.edu.iq

Abstract. After developing IoT devices, information security takes a critical role than any other period. Most IoT devices use weak passwords, insecure interface, poor management, and lack of patches and updates mechanism. To that end, researchers have used different techniques for building a system that can detect intrusions and ensure secured systems. This paper explored the most common types of attacks that threaten networks. Besides, it provides an overview of the existing datasets that researchers can use as benchmark datasets for evaluating their proposed approaches. Furthermore, we review the most significant works during the last ten years that have been introduced for building flow-based intrusion detection systems.

Keywords: Intrusion detection · Datasets · IoT security · Network Intrusion Detection System · Real-time detection

1 Introduction

In recent years, especially after the development of IoT devices, the number of handled devices increased massively. This increase certainly was accompanied by an increase in the number of attacks that threaten these devices [1]. Thus, developing an intrusion detection system (IDS) that can detect network threats and secure these resources becomes a big challenge in today's cyber world.

The conventional approach for these systems requires inspecting the payload of every packet for detecting unusual behaviors [2, 3]. Recently, researchers proposed an alternative approach as payload checking-based methods cannot be implemented with the high speeds that networks use today [4]. The proposed approach implies detecting the unusual behaviors from monitoring the features of the set of packets that pass through the network, like the pair of IP addresses, port numbers, and packet size. This type of system is called a flow-based intrusion detection system.

The flow-based IDS can be classified into a Misused-based system and an anomaly-based system according to the method used. Misuse-based systems recognize the attacks by storing signatures for each known attack. This method requires a continuous update for the signatures' database so that any new attacks or a deviation from an old attack can be detected. On the other hand, anomaly-based systems define the normal behavior

© Springer Nature Singapore Pte Ltd. 2022
S. R. Pokhrel et al. (Eds.): ATIS 2021, CCIS 1554, pp. 121–137, 2022.
https://doi.org/10.1007/978-981-19-1166-8_10

and consider any deviation from this predefined behavior as an attack. Regarding flow-based anomaly detection, a significant number of attempts were made. These works were examined using different machine learning (ML) algorithms, statistical approaches [5], and feature selection techniques [6]. The effectiveness of IDS can be evaluated from its ability to detect various attacks accurately.

To that end, researchers collected different datasets containing examples of normal and malicious records for evaluating IDSs, as it is difficult to label and evaluate the proposed approaches on live networks. However, these attempts could not develop an IDS that fulfills the requirements for zero-day attacks [7], where they either suffer from low detection accuracy or cannot detect the different types of attacks. In particular, they faced issues with detecting low-frequency attacks [6].

Several surveys were introduced in this field. An interesting example is a survey provided by Ansam Khraisat et al. [5], where the authors studied IDS approaches in general, including a misused-based systems and an anomaly-based systems. Besides, the benchmark datasets that are commonly used for evaluating these approaches were also studied. Furthermore, It presents the main evasion techniques used by attackers to avoid current intrusion detection systems. Another interesting attempt is [8], where the authors studied comprehensively the latest IDSs approaches. Especially, they focused on the approaches suggested to tackle the attacks that threaten the IoT model. Furthermore, the survey provides a deep insight to the IoT architecture, current vulnerabilities of this structure, and the relation of these vulnerabilities to the layers of the IoT architecture. The main contributions of this paper are summarized as follows: Firstly, it provides a comprehensive classification for different types of network attacks. Secondly, it provides an extensive comparison between the datasets that can be used as benchmark datasets in intrusion detection. Finally, it reviews the most interesting works in flow-based intrusion detection in the past ten years.

The rest of this paper is organized as follows. Section 2 gives an overview of the most common types of attacks, while Sect. 3 summarizes the existing datasets and compares their characteristics. On the other hand, Sect. 4 presents the previous attempts to build IDS and discusses these works' different aspects. Finally, conclusion points are given in Sect. 5.

2   Types of Attacks

Due to the diversity of network attacks, researchers proposed different taxonomies that classified these types based on their common properties. These works aimed to enable researchers in this field to build IDSs that can detect these different categories by choosing samples from the different groups. Here, we will present these attacks according to the taxonomy described in [9], where the authors classified the threats into five groups. The classification is based on the source of the attack, the targeted layer from the Open Systems Interconnection (OSI) model, and whether it is an active or passive attack.

Passive attacks are usually specialists in monitoring and gathering information without affecting any aspect of the media like spyware, adware, and different information gathering attacks. In contrast to passive attacks, active attacks degrade the performance, affect the media's data, and affect other media aspects. Examples of these attacks are

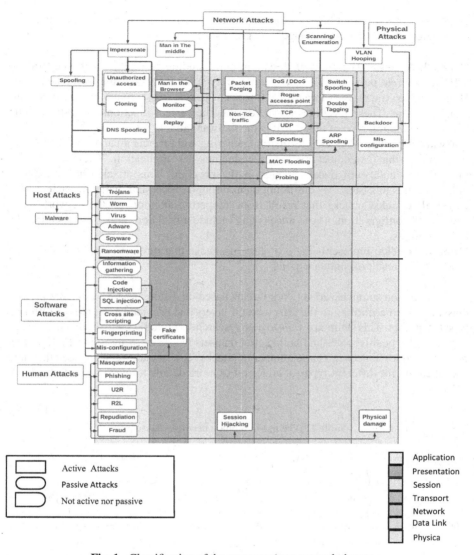

Fig. 1. Classification of the most common network threats.

viruses and Denial of Service (DoS). These attacks and their classification (active and passive attacks) are illustrated in "Fig. 1" where a rectangle box refers to active attacks while the oval shape refers to passive attacks. However, some attacks cannot be considered active or passive until their usage is known.

An example of such a type of attack is SQL injections. SQL injection is considered passive if it is used for querying data from a database. In contrast, it is considered active if it is used to alter data, drop tables, or alteration. The distribution of these attacks on the different OSI model layers is also illustrated in "Fig. 1 through colors where each color refers to a different layer. For example, grey refers to the application layer, while green refers to the transport layer. These groups are:

Network Attacks: The class of threats implies sending packets over the network to achieve different purposes. The most common type of this class is the DoS attack.
Host Attacks: the class of threats that attacks a specific host through executing a malicious program. These programs aim to disable the system functions or destroy them. The most common type of this threat is the malware attack.
Software Attacks: includes information gathering and probing attacks and code injection attacks that can inject malicious code into the application. The execution of this injected code will make changes in the program. This attack usually exploits vulnerabilities in systems by enforcing them through processing malicious statements.
Physical Attacks: attacks that result from tampering attempts on the network hardware or its configuration. These attacks can include a backdoor attack or changing the configurations.
Human Attacks: represents the last class of attacks that threaten networks. This type of attack is a result of human actions.

This section summarized network threats based on different bases. For example, we classified them according to the affected OSI layers and provided examples of different types of attacks. This summary aims to help researchers build IDS with higher accuracies and less false positive rates and build better datasets where we will see in "Table 1" that recent IDS does not cover a large number of attacks. To that end, we introduced the main classification for different types of attacks. For more details for each type of attack see [9].

Table 1. The most common network datasets

Reference	Dataset type	Year	Network traffic	Attacks types	Tools used	Number of features	Files format	Labeled observations
[17]	KDD99	1999	False	A1, A2, A3, A4	BRO-IDS tool	41	CSV files	Yes
[18]	Kyoto	2006	True	A5, A1, A6, A7, A8, A9	BRO-IDS tool	24	Sessions	Yes
[19]	DEFECON	2000	False	A8, A10	Only pcap (tcpdum) formats, without features generated from their traces are available		Pcap files	No
[20]	LBNL	2004/2005	True	A8		NA	Pcap files	No

(*continued*)

Table 1. (*continued*)

Reference	Dataset type	Year	Network traffic	Attacks types	Tools used	Number of features	Files format	Labeled observations
[21]	CAIDA	2008	True	A11		NA	Pcap (tcpdum) formats	No
[22]	UNIBS	2009	True	None		NA	Pcap files	Yes
[23]	NSLKDD	2009	False	A1, A2, A3, A4	BRO-IDS tool	41	ARFF and CSV format	Yes
[24]	CDX	2009	False	A10	The Snort IDS	248	Pcap files	No
[25]	DARPA	2009	True	A1, A11	The Tcptrace tool	11	Pcap files	No
[26]	MAWI	2010	True	22 class of A30, and A12	SiLK	29	Pcap files	Partially labelled
[27]	ISOT	2010	False	2 types of A13	Tcp replay tool	11	Pcap files	Yes
[28]	TUIDS	2011/2012	True	A13, A11, A8, A14, A15	The gulp and nfdump tools	50 packet features and 24 flow features	Tcpdump formats	Yes
[29]	ISCX	2012	True	A16, A1, A11, A15	The Snort, QRadar, OSSIM IDS management systems and ntop visualization systems	19	Pcap files	Yes
[30]	CTU-13	2013	True	7 types of A13	Argus NetFlow tool	13	Pcap files	Yes with BG
[31]	ADFA	2014	True	A17, A18, A19, A20, A21, A22	The Linux audited tool	26	Pcap files	Yes
[32]	SSHCure	2014	True	A23	NfSen (NetFlow Sensor)	7	Pcap files	Indirectly labeled
[33]	UNSW-NB15	2015	True	A24, A25, A1, A6, A26, A27, A28, A9, A29	Tcpdump and IXIA traffic generator Perfect Storm	49	CSV files	Yes, with BG
[13]	UGR'16	2016	True	A1, A3, A13, A31, A32, A33, A34	NetFlow traces	12	Nfcapd format	Yes with BG

(*continued*)

Table 1. (*continued*)

Reference	Dataset type	Year	Network traffic	Attacks types	Tools used	Number of features	Files format	Labeled observations
[34]	DDoS 2016	2016	False	A1, A4, 5 types of A11	A network simulator (NS2)	27	Pcap files	Yes
[35]	CICDS2017	2017	True	A13, A35, A15, A1, A11,A36, A16, A37, A38, A39	The Snort, QRadar, OSSIM IDS management systems and ntop visualization systems	80	Pcap files and CSV formats	Yes
[36]	NGIDS-DS	2017	True	A25, A1, A6, A26, A27, A9, A29	IXIA perfect-storm tool in Linux operating system	238	Pcap files	Yes
[37]	CSE-CIC -IDS2018	2018	True	A26, A1, A11, A15, A38, A16, A13	CICFlowMeter-V3 tool	84	CSV file and raw PCAP files	Yes

3 Types of Datasets

Dataset is an essential component in Network Intrusion Detection System (NIDS) as it is needed as a data source for evaluating the proposed approaches. Since it is difficult to label the normal and attack activities in live networks [10, 11], several researchers did their best to collect comprehensive real-time or off-line network data (contains a variety of normal and malicious records). Thus, to implement a NIDS, there are a lot of offline datasets that can be used as a data source. These datasets differ in their main characteristics, such as realistic, the number of missing records, and the number and types of included attacks. This section introduces the most common datasets used by researchers [12–16].

Table 1 shows a comprehensive comparison between the most common datasets. The comparison includes highlighting the types of attacks supported by each dataset and if these attacks observations were labeled. Besides, the number of attributes extracted from the packets of each data source and the tools used for this purpose were also investigated. Last but not least, the table shows the formats of each dataset file and stated if this data source represents realistic network traffic. The meaning of the symbols in the types of attacks column can be found in "Table 2".

The most commonly datasets that researchers have used as benchmark are the KDD CUP 99 dataset, NSL KDD dataset, and the UNSW-NB15 dataset. The first two datasets have multiple issues [6] and using these datasets will not represent a realistic output performance. However, researchers adopted these two datasets for a long time. On the other hand, the UNSW-NB15 dataset was recently collected as a benchmark dataset for evaluating the proposed approaches. This is a complex dataset representing realistic network traffic and contains the types of attacks that exist in the network today. After that, a series of datasets were published. However, these datasets have not been widely used. Thus, we will review only the datasets that have been widely used and adopted by researchers, such as DDoS 2016, UGR'16, CICIDS 2017, and CSE-CIC-IDS2018.

In addition to the mentioned datasets, Robertas Damasevicius et al. in [15] proposed a new dataset that represents the modern realistic network traffic to improve the existing methods in intrusion detection. The proposed dataset used data from real network traffic with labeled attack examples as opposed to the old ones that used artificially simulated attacks. This dataset was captured within ten months, and it offers 85 different features. These features enable us to detect 12 different types of attacks supported by the dataset. This dataset is publicly available, and researchers can use it as a benchmark dataset for evaluating their approaches. However, the forementioned datasets lack the information of IPv6, where the datasets contain only information of IPv4.

Table 2. The symbols used for the types of attacks

Symbol	Attack type	Symbol	Attack type	Symbol	Attack type
A1	DoS	A17	Hydra-FTP	A33	SSH scan
A2	U2R	A18	Hydra-SSH	A34	Spam anomaly
A3	R2L	A19	Adduser	A35	Cross-site scripting
A4	Probe	A20	Java-Meterpreter	A36	FTP
A5	Back scatter	A21	Meterpreter	A37	Heart bleed
A6	Exploits	A22	Web-shell	A38	Web attack
A7	Malware	A23	SSH attacks	A39	SQL injection
A8	Port scans	A24	Analysis	A40	LDDoS
A9	Shellcode	A25	Backdoors	A41	Flash crowd
A10	Buffer overflow	A26	Generic	A42	IP sweep
A11	DDoS	A27	Reconnaissance	A43	Neptune
A12	Flooding	A28	Fuzzers	A44	Nmap
A13	Botnet	A29	Worms	A45	Satan
A14	Coordinated port scan	A30	Scanning	A46	Tripping
A15	SSH brute force	A31	IP in blacklist	A47	Relay
A16	Infiltrating the network from the inside	A32	UDP scan	A48	Injection

Table 3. Comparison between previous approaches in intrusion detection

Article	Year	Dataset	Number of features	Technique	Attacks types	Strength	Weakness	Results
[38]	2011	MAWI	1	The least mean square (LMS) filter with Pearson chi-square divergence	23 type of A11	Accurately detects a low intensity attacks, thus it is suitable for high speed networks	Can achieve such a high DR at the cost of computational complexity and the memory size required	100% detection Rate (DR)
[39]	2011	KDD CUP 99	11	Finite generalized Dirichlet mixture models, in the context. of Bayesian variational inference	A1, A2, A3 and A4	Shows high accuracy, low FPR, and small average cost in comparison with KNN, SVM, the neural networks, and TCM-KNN approaches	The DRs for R2L and U2R classes…. is low because of a shortage of training set for these classes	DRs are 96.5%,75.4%, 69.6% and 85.1%, respectively
[40]	2012	Real flow data	1	Congestion Participation Rate-based approach	4 types of A40	Detects effectively all types of LDDoS attacks in comparison with DFT-based approach	The memory size required needs to be further reduced using MBF techniques	Can achieve 100% DR with 1.625% FPR at a specified CPRvalue
[41]	2013	KDD CUP 99	41	Multivariate correlation analysis (MCA) and further enhanced by triangle-area-based technique	6 types of A1	Detects different Dos attacks with high DR. Needs less computational complexity and approximately half the time in comparison with two approaches from the literature	DRs are 71.50% for Teardrop, 82.44% for Neptune, 0.00% for Land attack	DA is 99.95% and nearly 100.00% DRs for most DoS attacks

(continued)

Table 3. (*continued*)

Article	Year	Dataset	Number of features	Technique	Attacks types	Strength	Weakness	Results
[42]	2013	KDD CUP 99	3	Optimized Bayesian filters in series	A1, A2, A3, A4	Realistic and practical method detects R2L and U2R attack with superior DR in comparison with what Chou achieved in his Ph.D. dissertation	The overall system's DR needs to be enhanced. Authors suggest for this purpose and to make the system capture the new attacks besides to the known types of attacks	96.85% for R2L attack
[43]	2013	Real flow data	4	Exponentially Weighted Moving Average (EWMA) and CUSUM	A12	Detects anomalies in near-real-time (in a few seconds) with only 5% additional CPU time and with negligible memory usage	Detects only large flooding attacks (high-intensity attacks). Thus, the FPR needs to be further reduced	92% DR with 6% FPR
[44]	2013	MAWI	3	ADMIRE	22 class of A30 and A12	ADMIRE uses extra sketch step which makes it outperforms other PCA-based methods such as gamma and KL methods from different metrics of performance measure	DR needs to be further increased	TPR of 0.1901and FPR. Of 0.0021and DA of 0.0589
[45]	2015	Real flow data	7	Principal component analysis (PCA)	A1, A11	Detects the mentioned attacks with 3 s detection delay and with reduced computational resources	The FAR needs to be further reduced, cannot detect port scans, probing, U2R and R2L	DR larger than 90%

(*continued*)

Table 3. (continued)

Article	Year	Dataset	Number of features	Technique	Attacks types	Strength	Weakness	Results
[46]	2015	KDD CUP 99	6	2 Stage Novelty Detection and Reaction (2SNDR) algorithm	A42, A43, A44, A45 and A1	Accurate, fast, and shows higher performance in terms of accuracy in comparison with two significant methods	Needs adjustment by using Bayesian inference for being efficient for application in real networks	98.4% DA
[47]	2015	KDD CUP 99	15	improved Naïve Bayes algorithm based on PCA	A1, A2, A3, A4	Obvious improvement in DR over the traditional Naïve Bayes algorithm and neural network method	Their experimental dataset doesn't represent realistic network traffic, most of the attacks that is supported in the dataset do not exist now	DRs values range between 98% and 78% for the different attacks
[48]	2015	KDD CUP 99 and the UNSW-NB15	12 Feature as an average for each type	Association Rule Mining algorithm (ARM), as a feature selection algorithm along with Naïve Bayes (NB) classifier and Expectation-Maximization (EM), as a clustering technique	A1, A2, A3, A4, A25, A6, A24, A26, A28, A9, A27, A29	Reduce the number of KDD CUP 99 dataset features and improves the detection performance	Cannot detect several record categories in the UNSW-NB15 dataset because of the similarity of the values of these records, and hence a better method must be used for finding best features	For the KDD CUP 99 dataset the best results are 78.06% DA and 22.08% FAR while for the UNSW-NB15 dataset 37.5% DA and 62.58% FAR

(continued)

Table 3. (*continued*)

Article	Year	Dataset	Number of features	Technique	Attacks types	Strength	Weakness	Results
[49]	2015	UNSW-NB15	10	Collaborative anomaly detection framework (CADF)	A24, A25, A1, A6, A26, A27, A28, A9 and A29	Detects the mentioned attacks with good DR, doesn't need high processing time, simply computed with less computational resources compared to three peer techniques	DR needs to be further increased and FPR needs to be further decreased	95.6% DR and 3.5% FPR
[50]	2016	CPS and UNSW-NB15	9 and 9	Beta Mixture Hidden Markov Mechanism (MHMM)	A46, A47, A48, A24, A25, A1, A6, A26, A27, A28, A9 and A29	Detects the mentioned attacks with high DR and low FPR and processing time in comparison with five peer techniques	The detection rate for the UNSW-NB15 and the detection delay 55 s still needs further improvement	DRs of 98.12% and 95.89% and FPRs of 2.21% and 3.82% Respectively
[51]	2017	NSL-KDD and the UNSW-NB15	8 and 8	Finite dirichlet mixture models, (DMM-based ADS)	A1, A2, A3, A4	Scalable, outperforms three existing techniques, in terms of DRs and FPRs	Cannot detect attack type because it is designed to handle binary classification (normal or attacks)	97.8% and 93.9% DRs, and 2.5 and 5.8 FPRs respectively
[52]	2017	NSL-KDD and the UNSW-NB15	20 and 20	A novel two-stage method based on Reduced Error Pruning Tree (REPTree) algorithm	A1, A2, A3, A4, A25, A6, A24, A26, A28, A9, A27, A29	The method shows a lower detection delay, reduced the number of used features to the half with a simple improvement in the accuracy	The accuracy still needs further improvement	89.85% and 88.95% DAs

(*continued*)

Table 3. (continued)

Article	Year	Dataset	Number of features	Technique	Attacks types	Strength	Weakness	Results
[53]	2017	KDD CUP 99 and the UNSW-NB15	18 and 20	The wrapper approach is based on a genetic algorithm along with logistic regression GA-LR and Decision Tree classifier (DT)	A1, A2, A3, A4, A25, A6, A24, A26, A28, A9, A27, A29	The method shows good results with the KDDCUP 99 dataset	The method fails with the UNSW-NB15 dataset and this reflects the complexity of this dataset	Accuracies of 99.90% and 81.42% respectively
[54]	2018	UNSW-NB15	8	New beta mixture model (BMM-ADS)	A1, A25, A6, A24, A26, A28, A9, A27, A29	High performance in detecting the mentioned attacks in comparison with three recent Mechanisms	Requires a huge number of instances to be properly learned, the performance needs to be enhanced	92.7% DR and 5.9% FPR
[55]	2018	NIMS and UNSW-NB15	16 and 12	ensemble learning method using Artificial Neural Network (ANN), DT, and NB classifiers	A1, A25, A6, A24, A26, A28, A9, A27, A29	Shows very high accuracy in detecting all the types of attacks with the HTTP protocol. Besides, very high accuracies were also got with the DNS protocol	Couldn't detect the types of attack that exist with a few numbers of records like Analysis, Backdoor, and Worms	Very high accuracies in detecting all types. 0% detection accuracy for Analysis, Backdoor, and Worms
[56]	2019	UNSW-NB15	5	Gradient Boost Machine, LR, and SVM as a first stage and NB, DT, and multinomial SVM as a second stage	A1, A25, A6, A24, A26, A28, A9, A27, A29	Proposed a two stage detection method which results in an improvement in the results	Fails to detect Analysis, Backdoor, Shellcode, and Worms attacks. The authors explained that the reasons are not enough records or the features that exist in this dataset are not enough	86.04% DA for multi-label classification

(continued)

Table 3. (*continued*)

Article	Year	Dataset	Number of features	Technique	Attacks types	Strength	Weakness	Results
[57]	2019	KDD CUP 99, Kyoto 2006,and UNSW-NB15	13, NA, and NA	correlation-based feature selection technique and particle swarm optimization with different classifiers SVM, kNN, and NB	A1, A2, A3, A4, A5, A6, A7, A8, A9, A25, A24, A26, A28, A9, A27, A29	Improves the performance when used with KDD CUP 99, and Kyoto 2006	The method's accuracy when applied to UNSW-NB15 needs further improvement	DAs of 99.9291%, 99.752%, and 92.2151% respectively with SVM
[58]	2020	UNSW-NB15	30	Gain Ratio (GR) as a feature selection and multi-layer perception neural network as a classifier	A1, A25, A6, A24, A26, A28, A9, A27, A29	Applied GR and reduce the number of features to 30	The DA needs improvement and another methods is needed to reduce the features of this dataset	76.96% DA
[59]	2020	NSL-KDD and UNSW-NB15	24 and 16	improved multi-objective immune algorithm (MOIA) with the neural network	A1, A2, A3, A4, A25, A6, A24, A26, A28, A9, A27, A29	Shows an acceptable performance in detecting NSL-KDD dataset	The DA was very low in detecting UNSW-NB15 dataset attacks except for the Generic attack which exists frequently	99.47% and 79.81% Das respectively
[6]	2021	UNSW-NB15	20	Forward Selection Ranking and Backward Elimination Ranking along with DT and Random forest classifier	A1, A25, A6, A24, A26, A28, A9, A27, A29	Detects all the types of attacks with high accuracy including low-frequency attacks	The work suggested the subset of features for detecting each type of attacks separately and the subset of features for binary classifying the data but it wasn't able to identify the types of attacks	99.965% DA in binary classifying the data

4   A Review of Intrusion Detection Approaches

Several attempts were made in the field of flow-based intrusion detection. These attempts examined different techniques to design an efficient system that can detect malicious events in near real-time. These approaches include classification, clustering, deep learning, statistical-based, and different features reduction techniques.

This section reviews the most significant approaches proposed by researchers during the past ten years for building a flow-based intrusion detection system. Besides, we highlight the strength and weaknesses of each of these works. This study are presented in "Table 3" The meaning of the symbols in the types of attacks column can be found in "Table 2".

The metrics we use for evaluating these works are as follows: detection delay (the ability of the system to detect attacks in real-time), the characteristics of the used dataset (such as realistic network traffic and contains the types of threats that exists in the network today), number and types of detected attacks, Detection Accuracy (DA) and False Positive Rate (FPR) values. For the works that used features selection techniques, we use the following metrics for evaluating them: number of features, computational complexity, and the required memory size.

In summary, it is noted that high accuracies with low FPRs were achieved in detecting most of the attacks, especially with the types of network attacks that exist with high intensity. However, these systems suffer from high computational complexity and large memory size. Furthermore, most of the proposed systems show a high detection delay, fail to detect the types of attacks that exist with a low number of records, fail in identifying the type of attack (multi-label classification), especially with current complex datasets. Most attempts, especially on the recent complex datasets, where there were unable to select the features that enable the detection of all types of attacks or achieve this aim with a high number of features.

5   Conclusion

In this paper, we have provided an overview of the existing types of network threats and divided these types into groups with similar properties to give the researchers the chance to detect these categories by choosing a sample of attacks from the different groups. Besides, we have comprehensively studied the existing benchmark datasets to help researchers choose a dataset that represents realistic network traffic, and contains the types of attacks that exist in the network today, provided by labels for the normal and malicious observations. Furthermore, we have reviewed the different approaches proposed by researchers for building flow-based intrusion detection systems and evaluated these works according to the suggested metrics. From this review, we have shown the gaps in the existing IDSs.

Future work will investigate building a lightweight flow-based IDS with a higher DA and lower FPR. Especially for the types of attacks that exist with low intensity and can achieve such performance with a small detection delay (a few seconds) with the fewest possible number of features. In addition, the proposed system must detect the new upcoming attacks or the deviation from the old attacks from monitoring the changes in the underlying system behavior.

References

1. Alturfi, S.M., Marhoon, H.A., Al-Musawi, B.: Internet of Things security techniques: a survey. In: AIP Conference Proceedings. AIP Publishing LLC. (2020)
2. Roesch, M.: Snort, intrusion detection system (2008). http://www.snort.org/. TH Project, Tools http://project.honeynet.org/tools/index
3. Paxson, V.: Bro: a system for detecting network intruders in real-time. Comput. Netw. 31(23–24), 2435–2463 (1999)
4. Sperotto, A., et al.: An overview of IP flow-based intrusion detection. IEEE Commun. Surv. Tut. 12(3), 343–356 (2010)
5. Khraisat, A., Gondal, I., Vamplew, P., Kamruzzaman, J.: Survey of intrusion detection systems: techniques, datasets and challenges. Cybersecurity 2(1), 1–22 (2019). https://doi.org/10.1186/s42400-019-0038-7
6. Al-Bakaa, A., Al-Musawi, B.: Improving the performance of intrusion detection system through finding the most effective features. In: 2021 International Congress of Advanced Technology and Engineering (ICOTEN). IEEE (2021)
7. AL-Musawi, B.Q.M.: Mitigating DoS/DDoS attacks using IPTables. Int. J. Eng. Technol. 12(3), 101–111 (2012)
8. Elrawy, M.F., Awad, A.I., Hamed, H.F.A.: Intrusion detection systems for IoT-based smart environments: a survey. J. Cloud Comput. 7(1), 1–20 (2018)
9. Hindy, H., et al.: A taxonomy and survey of intrusion detection system design techniques, network threats and datasets (2018)
10. Patcha, A., Park, J.-M.: An overview of anomaly detection techniques: existing solutions and latest technological trends. Comput. Netw. 51(12), 3448–3470 (2007)
11. Vasudevan, A., Harshini, E., Selvakumar, S.: SSENet-2011: a network intrusion detection system dataset and its comparison with KDD CUP 99 dataset. In: 2011 2nd Asian Himalayas International Conference on Internet (AH-ICI). IEEE (2011)
12. Moustafa, N., Hu, J., Slay, J.: A holistic review of network anomaly detection systems: a comprehensive survey. J. Netw. Comput. Appl. 128, 33–55 (2019)
13. Maciá-Fernández, G., et al.: UGR '16: a new dataset for the evaluation of cyclostationarity-based network IDSs. Comput. Secur. 73, 411–424 (2018)
14. Umer, M.F., Sher, M., Bi, Y.: Flow-based intrusion detection: techniques and challenges. Comput. Secur. 70, 238–254 (2017)
15. Damasevicius, R., et al.: LITNET-2020: an annotated real-world network flow dataset for network intrusion detection. Electronics 9(5), 800 (2020)
16. Ring, M., et al.: A survey of network-based intrusion detection data sets. Comput. Secur. 86, 147–167 (2019)
17. Kddcup 1999 (1999). http://kdd.ics.uci.edu/databases
18. Song, J., et al.: Statistical analysis of honeypot data and building of Kyoto 2006+ dataset for NIDS evaluation. In: Proceedings of the 1st Workshop on Building Analysis Datasets and Gathering Experience Returns for Security (2011)
19. Defcon dataset (2000). https://www.defcon.org/html/links/dc-ctf.html
20. LBNL dataset (2005). http://powerdata.lbl.gov/download.html
21. CAIDA dataset (2008). https://www.caida.org/data/
22. Gringoli, F., et al.: Gt: picking up the truth from the ground for internet traffic. ACM SIGCOMM Comput. Commun. Rev. 39(5), 12–18 (2009)
23. Tavallaee, M., et al.: A detailed analysis of the KDD CUP 99 data set. In: 2009 IEEE Symposium on Computational Intelligence for Security and Defense Applications. IEEE (2009)

24. Sangster, B., et al.: Toward instrumenting network warfare competitions to generate labeled datasets. In: CSET (2009)
25. DARPA 2009 dataset (2009). https://www.predict.org/
26. Fontugne, R., et al.: MAWILab: combining diverse anomaly detectors for automated anomaly labeling and performance benchmarking. In: Proceedings of the 6th International Conference (2010)
27. Saad, S., et al.: Detecting P2P botnets through network behavior analysis and machine learning. In: 2011 9th Annual International Conference on Privacy, Security and Trust. IEEE (2011)
28. Gogoi, P., Bhuyan, M.H., Bhattacharyya, D.K., Kalita, J.K.: Packet and flow based network intrusion dataset. In: Parashar, M., Kaushik, D., Rana, O.F., Samtaney, R., Yang, Y., Zomaya, A. (eds.) IC3 2012. CCIS, vol. 306, pp. 322–334. Springer, Heidelberg (2012). https://doi.org/10.1007/978-3-642-32129-0_34
29. Shiravi, A., et al.: Toward developing a systematic approach to generate benchmark datasets for intrusion detection. Comput. Secur. **31**(3), 357–374 (2012)
30. Garcia, S., et al.: An empirical comparison of botnet detection methods. Comput. Secur. **45**, 100–123 (2014)
31. ADFA dataset (2014). https://www.unsw.adfa.edu.au/australian-centre-for-cyber-security/cybersecurity/ADFA-IDS-Datasets/
32. Hofstede, R., et al.: SSH compromise detection using NetFlow/IPFIX. ACM SIGCOMM Comput. Commun. Rev. **44**(5), 20–26 (2014)
33. Moustafa, N., Slay, J.: UNSW-NB15: a comprehensive data set for network intrusion detection systems (UNSW-NB15 network data set). In: 2015 Military Communications and Information Systems Conference (MilCIS). IEEE (2015)
34. Alkasassbeh, M., et al.: Detecting distributed denial of service attacks using data mining techniques. Int. J. Adv. Comput. Sci. Appl. **7**(1), 436–445 (2016)
35. Sharafaldin, I., Lashkari, A.H., Ghorbani, A.A.: Toward generating a new intrusion detection dataset and intrusion traffic characterization. ICISSp **1**, 108–116 (2018)
36. Haider, W., et al.: Generating realistic intrusion detection system dataset based on fuzzy qualitative modeling. J. Netw. Comput. Appl. **87**, 185–192 (2017)
37. CSE-CIC-IDS2018 dataset (2018). https://www.unb.ca/cic/datasets/ids-2018.html
38. Salem, O., et al.: Flooding attacks detection in traffic of backbone networks. In: 2011 IEEE 36th Conference on Local Computer Networks. IEEE (2011)
39. Fan, W., Bouguila, N., Ziou, D.: Unsupervised anomaly intrusion detection via localized bayesian feature selection. In: 2011 IEEE 11th International Conference on Data Mining. IEEE (2011)
40. Zhang, C., et al.: Flow level detection and filtering of low-rate DDoS. Comput. Netw. **56**(15), 3417–3431 (2012)
41. Tan, Z., et al.: A system for denial-of-service attack detection based on multivariate correlation analysis. IEEE Trans. Parallel Distrib. Syst. **25**(2), 447–456 (2013)
42. Altwaijry, H.: Bayesian based intrusion detection system. In: Kim, H., Ao, S.I., Rieger, B. (eds.) IAENG Transactions on Engineering Technologies. Lecture Notes in Electrical Engineering, vol. 170, pp. 29–44. Springer, Dordrecht (2013). https://doi.org/10.1007/978-94-007-4786-9_3
43. Hofstede, R., et al.: Towards real-time intrusion detection for NetFlow and IPFIX. In: Proceedings of the 9th International Conference on Network and Service Management, CNSM 2013. IEEE (2013)
44. Kanda, Y., et al.: ADMIRE: anomaly detection method using entropy-based PCA with three-step sketches. Comput. Commun. **36**(5), 575–588 (2013)

45. Fernandes, G., Jr., Rodrigues, J.J., Proenca, M.L., Jr.: Autonomous profile-based anomaly detection system using principal component analysis and flow analysis. Appl. Soft Comput. **34**, 513–525 (2015)
46. Gruhl, C., et al.: A building block for awareness in technical systems: online novelty detection and reaction with an application in intrusion detection. In: 2015 IEEE 7th International Conference on Awareness Science and Technology (iCAST). IEEE (2015)
47. Han, X., et al.: A Naive Bayesian network intrusion detection algorithm based on principal component analysis. In: 2015 7th International Conference on Information Technology in Medicine and Education (ITME). IEEE (2015)
48. Moustafa, N., Slay, J.: The significant features of the UNSW-NB15 and the KDD99 data sets for network intrusion detection systems. In: 2015 4th International Workshop on Building Analysis Datasets and Gathering Experience Returns for Security (BADGERS). IEEE (2015)
49. Moustafa, N., et al.: Collaborative anomaly detection framework for handling big data of cloud computing. In: 2017 Military Communications and Information Systems Conference (MilCIS). IEEE (2017)
50. Moustafa, N., et al.: A new threat intelligence scheme for safeguarding Industry 4.0 systems. IEEE Access **6**, 32910–32924 (2018)
51. Moustafa, N., Creech, G., Slay, J.: Big data analytics for intrusion detection system: statistical decision-making using finite dirichlet mixture models. In: Carrascosa, I.P., Kalutarage, H.K., Huang, Y. (eds.) Data analytics and decision support for cybersecurity. DA, pp. 127–156. Springer, Cham (2017). https://doi.org/10.1007/978-3-319-59439-2_5
52. Belouch, M., El Hadaj, S., Idhammad, M.: A two-stage classifier approach using REPTree algorithm for network intrusion detection. Int. J. Adv. Comput. Sci. Appl. **8**(6), 389–394 (2017)
53. Khammassi, C., Krichen, S.: A GA-LR wrapper approach for feature selection in network intrusion detection. Comput. Secur. **70**, 255–277 (2017)
54. Moustafa, N., Creech, G., Slay, J.: Anomaly detection system using beta mixture models and outlier detection. In: Pattnaik, P.K., Rautaray, S.S., Das, H., Nayak, J. (eds.) Progress in Computing, Analytics and Networking. AISC, vol. 710, pp. 125–135. Springer, Singapore (2018). https://doi.org/10.1007/978-981-10-7871-2_13
55. Moustafa, N., Turnbull, B., Choo, K.-K.R.: An ensemble intrusion detection technique based on proposed statistical flow features for protecting network traffic of internet of things. IEEE Internet Things J. **6**(3), 4815–4830 (2018)
56. Meftah, S., Rachidi, T., Assem, N.: Network based intrusion detection using the UNSW-NB15 dataset. Int. J. Comput. Digit. Syst. **8**(5), 478–487 (2019)
57. Ahmad, T., Aziz, M.N.: Data preprocessing and feature selection for machine learning intrusion detection systems. ICIC Exp. Lett. **13**(2), 93–101 (2019)
58. Mebawondu, J.O., Alowolodu, O.D., Mebawondu, J.O., Adetunmbi, A.O.: Network intrusion detection system using supervised learning paradigm. Sci. Afr. **9**, e00497 (2020)
59. Wei, W., et al.: A multi-objective immune algorithm for intrusion feature selection. Appl. Soft Comput. **95**, 106522 (2020)

Cloud and IoT

Chapter XVI

A Novel SDN-Based IOT Security Architecture Model for Big Data

Ojaswi Bhimineni⬤, Geda Sai Venkata Abhijith⬤, and Srikanth Prabhu(✉)⬤

Department of Computer Science and Engineering, Manipal Institute of Technology, Manipal, Karnataka, India
srikanth.prabhu@manipal.edu

Abstract. In this paper, A Novel SDN-Based IoT Security Architecture Model for Big Data is implemented. To control and manage the network, Software Defined Networking (SDN) is used. The main intent of SDN controller is to implement a protocol for controlling the devices linearly and in the same way to modify the protocol for improving the performance. The entire novel SDN based IOT architecture is divided into four layers, mainly application layer, transport layer, gateway layer and data plane layer. Application layer consists of security, network update and quality of services. This mainly depends on the SDN (software Defined Network). Transport layer consists of wired communication network, mobile communication network and SDN controller. Gateway layer uses SDN gateway controller. Data plane communication protocol will provide communication for the protocol. Data plane will perform the physical switch, virtual switch and network devices. From results, it can observe that it gives effective results in terms of efficiency and performance.

Keywords: Software-Defined Networking (SDN) · IOT (Internet of Things) · CPU (Central Processing Unit) · Distributing network · Efficiency · Performance

1 Introduction

As one of the new ways to deal with make network setup simpler and to understand a more adaptable organization climate, Software-Defined Networking (SDN) has developed [1]. In SDN, network gadgets for example switches which are particular for bundle sending, while the control work is isolated from sending plane. The control work is executed in a SDN controller that deals with all organization gadgets set on the sending plane through a product program.

In this way, the regulator recovers the organization data from all organization gadgets and cycles the data fittingly to choose bundle sending rules. SDN is obtained, by isolating the control and information planes, handling the unpredictability, firmness of the customary organization. SDN empowers associations to deal with their networks in an automatic way and to scale the organizations without subverting client experience, dependability, and execution. Through the SDN approach, network directors are not needed to actualize custom conventions and arrangements on every gadget independently inside the organization [2, 3].

© Springer Nature Singapore Pte Ltd. 2022
S. R. Pokhrel et al. (Eds.): ATIS 2021, CCIS 1554, pp. 141–148, 2022.
https://doi.org/10.1007/978-981-19-1166-8_11

For the most part, SDN design control-plane capacities are portrayed from actual gadgets and are worked by an outside regulàtor (for example, a standard worker running SDN programming). The SDN approach has the capability of encouraging the consolidation and arrangement of new gadgets into the current design. The SDN regulator, by taking favorable position of its all-encompassing perspective on the organization, improves the traffic designing limits of the organization administrators through video traffic.

This will express the issues as (1) a regulator stores the entirety of the data for example, the actual geography, the worldwide organization status and the arrangements into a social information base and (2) each utilitarian part can work autonomously and non-concurrently to forestall clashes brought by the data refreshes [4]. A vital thought of the framework is to oversee modern data about the organization arrangement or the organization status in information bases.

The information base has the upside of information handling and addresses non concurrent refreshes by the exchange preparing. Each utilitarian part brings the data put away in data bases and makes data about organization arrangement. Every segment works autonomously and non-concurrently through information bases, since the way calculation work is isolated from the control work.

For this reason, it additionally considers table structures of the information bases that store the organization data, for example, the actual geography and bundle sending rules. To uncover favorable circumstances of our methodology, it will apply the idea of information base arranged administration on an Open Flow-based trial organize and approve that this framework can design an Open Flow-based organization through the data sets [5].

The organization establishes different gadgets such as switches, numerous activities. Though, they are unequipped to deal with the organization in instance of connection disappointment. They battle extremely difficult to change over elevated level arrangement as indicated by the altering states of the organization with limited apparatuses. SDN has solution to this issue by providing the organization engineering which bolsters the plane of segment.

For parcel move smooth working the information, control plane is decoupled. The SDN execution is carried out by a convention known as Open-Flow that decouple the plane, shows in determination manner to transmit the information. It gives an open interface between the two planes. On account of the unified control in the Open-flow organization, it turns out to be very simple to convey steering procedures to the switch. The information consists of switch and control plane comprises of regulator. The sending plane for example information plane is liable for the transmission of information and control plane figures strategy for transferring of data.

The knowledge of the entirety network is moved to the concentrated programming based SDN regulator, which acts like manager. The change, control, and checking of communicated information is being finished by the SDN control segments.

Conventional organizations interfacing a large portion of the present web have demonstrated to advance gradually which are restricted in usefulness and have a moderately significant level of Operation Expenditures (OPEX) because of manual upkeep and organization, and are, in nature, generally static to gadget disappointments and stream changes. Then again, worker virtualization and distributed computing have made the worker side of the Data Center more adaptable and versatile to the ever developing and changing applications worker necessities.

Applications are currently ready to be served by high quantities of virtual machines that can rapidly scale in CPU and memory assets. This scene has put conventional organizations at the center of attention, situating them as a bottleneck for application organization and versatility. Along these lines, as of now media communications specialist cooperation and IT associations, as a rule, are under expanding strain to be more proficient than any time in recent memory.

Another systems administration worldview, Software-Defined Networking (SDN) is used to help and defeat the adaptability and versatility restrictions of conventional systems administration by making use of organization board centralization and by cultivating robotization utilizing network programmability. Despite the fact that the possibility of a programmable organization isn't new, SDN has become an interesting issue in the systems administration network. Programming Defined Networking is as of now changing the manner in which a few associations convey and deal with their organizations. Microsoft, Amazon, Google and Face book among others, who run the vast majority of the web traffic today are early adopters of SDN and drivers of a few SDN activities.

2   SDN Application in Various Field

2.1   Internet of Things (IOTs)

The converging of SDN and IOT bring energizing stages. SDN has the ability to flawlessly convey the traffic and handle the billions of information arising out of the gadget that is being connected to the IOT. SDN follows the division cycle to deal with the information emerging from the network. It isolates the total IOT network into little sections and each part can be constrained by various regulators in order to make the network work run easily. SDN connected IOT network serves better for security worries as it has the worldwide perspective on the organization.

2.2   Other Systems Administration Gadgets

They proposed an engineering that depends on the idea of SDN to determine the discontinuity difficulties of the home organization by adjusting the concentrated approach. It proposed another kind of gadget that understands the home systems administration gadgets dependent on the inclination for interactive media applications. This proposed innovation gives high adaptability in arranging gadgets and controlling, it encourages the clients to depend on the product applications as opposed to rely on the manual arranging of numerous clients.

2.3   Distributed Computing

The quantity of information delivered by the organization is too enormous to deal with. It offers ascend to the idea of cloud, networks make cloud. Due to the enormous space required for putting away applications, these applications may need to change in cloud. SDN makes it conceivable by the help of unified regulator which is arranged by programming related conventions.

Remote and Versatile Organization

The commitment of SDN in remote organization is known as SDN for example programming characterized remote organization. The specialists have considered about the Open-stream proposed by whitepaper. Open-stream depends on the Ethernet switch, comprise of stream table with the limit of adding or then again eliminating stream sections.

Organization of SDN in remote organization gives consistent handover between various remote advances by inserting of Open-street. SDN underpins the stream driven model that helps in settling the issue of hub relocation by executing capacities and making it configurable at higher layer. The SDN design is open and sharable between various specialist organizations and utilize proving ground utilizing Open-stream, Wifi and WiMAX.

3 Literature Survey

In customary systems administration, the organization transport conventions, the dispersed control inside the switches and switches comprise the key advancements that empower data to travel across the globe through computerized bundles. Hence their broad appropriation, customary IP networks are hard to oversee as well as perplexing (Silvio E. Quincozes, 2017) [6]. For articulation of the necessary elevated level organization plan and strategies into an ongoing parcel sending organization, network administrators should re-arrange each organization gadget with specific seller low-level orders.

Software Defined Networking (SDN) (Mckeown, 2016) (Schenker, 2016) [7] is another organizing worldview, which offers any expectation of changing the down sides related with existing organization models. First, it disentangles the vertical mix through partition of an organization's control plane (control rationale) from basic switches and switches, which forward the information plane (traffic).

Second, utilizing the outline of the information and control planes, organization switches are disentangled into sending gadgets, consequently encouraging the execution of the control rationale in a brought together rationale regulator, disentangling network advancement, arrangement, and strategy implementation (Kim and Feamster, 2016) [8].

In spite of the fact that Open Flow and SDN started as scholastic tests, they picked up impressive footing in the business in the ongoing years. Numerous business switch sellers presently fuse Open Flow API uphold inside their hardware. The SDN force constrained Deutsche Telekom, Verizon, Microsoft, Yahoo, Face book, and Google and Open Networking Foundation (ONF) to advance and embrace SDN through open limits improvement. As the early issues with the adaptability of SDN were handled. From that point forward, SDN ideas have developed from scholastic activities toward business achievement.

For example, Google has introduced a programming characterized network for interconnecting its Data Centers in the whole world. Google creation SDN network has been operational for a time of 3 years, in this manner empowering the firm to decrease expenses and improve operational productivity. (Jain, et al., 2015) [9]. Another model can be found in VMware SDN arrangement gives an elevated level working programmable organization without straightforwardly depending in individual basic organizing devices however in a pool of accessible equipment and in light of on the organization deliberation rule of SDN.

Finally, the biggest IT firms on the planet for example, Cisco, Facebook, Google, or Juniper have joined the SDN normalization consortia Open Day light, ODL (Open Day light), another show of the SDN from the modern perspective.

In a SDN plan, the control plane is brought together in an organization regulator. The organization regulator can give a preoccupied perspective on the whole systems administration framework permitting the organization chairman to utilize custom conventions/arrangements over the organization equipment.

The organization regulator is the organization working framework liable for finding the ongoing condition of all the organization gadgets associated with its southward interface and ensure that they are performing as indicated by the organization approaches learned from the application layer by means of the northward interface.

As clarified by Gude et al., (2015) [10] a key highlight of the organization working framework is its capacity to empower the board applications to be composed as brought together projects over elevated level names conversely to the time-consuming conveyed calculations over low-level delivers used to arrange heritage networks (Gude, et al., n.d.).

4   A Novel SDN-Based IOT Security Architecture Model

The below Fig. 1 shows the architecture of Novel SDN-Based IoT Security architecture Model. In this the entire architecture is application layer, transport layer, gate away layer and data plane. Application layer consists of security, network update and quality of services. This mainly depends on the SDN (software Defined Network).

Transport layer consists of wired communication network, mobile communication network and SDN controller. Gate away layer uses SDN gateway controller. Data plane communication protocol will provide communication for the protocol. Data plane will perform the physical switch, virtual switch and network devices.

The data from perception layer is transmitted by transport layer. Usually collected data from perception layer is transmitted to application layer through the technologies of wireless communication, WAN communications and mobile.

Application layer is the practical IOT application embodiment. Based on specific requirements it processes, analyzes the data from transport layer, it controls, takes correct decisions and provides intelligent applications, feedback services for fulfilling the actual requirements like smart transportation, smart home, smart city, smart logistics, etc.

In this paper gate way layer is researched is the major key for integrating IoT, SDN technology. Controller manages the gateway layer. Data packet is analyzed for find out whether it is transmitted to transport layer or not. If it identifies the security threat, then it discards the data packet and is not transmitted. In this technique, decision- making, security of data and checking are put forwarded from application layer or conventional transport layer to gate way layer.

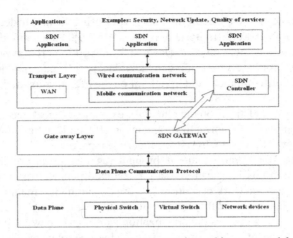

Fig. 1. Novel SDN-based IOT security architecture model

By the above process secure data will be only transmitted to transport layer and next to application layer that protects the IoT risk greatly from threatened. In the network it can also reduce the transmitted amount of data. The gateway layer security policy is configured dynamically and adjusted based on controller measurement rules.

5   Results

The below Fig. 2 shows the comparison of efficiency for SDN controller and Novel SDN based IOT security architecture. Compared to SDN controller, Novel SDN based IOT architecture security will improve the efficiency in very effective way.

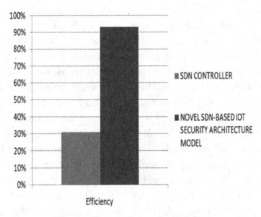

Fig. 2. Comparison of efficiency

The below Fig. 3 shows the comparison of reliability for SDN controller and Novel SDN based IOT security architecture. Compared to SDN controller, Novel SDN based IOT security architecture will improve the reliability of system in very effective way.

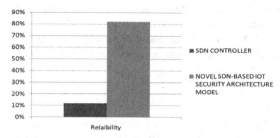

Fig. 3. Comparison of reliability

The below Fig. 4 shows the comparison of computational time for SDN controller and Novel SDN based IOT security architecture. Compared to SDN controller, Novel SDN based IOT security architecture will reduce the computational time of system in very effective way (Table 1).

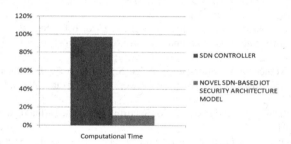

Fig. 4. Comparison of computational time

Table 1. Parameters of novel SDN based IOT security architecture

S. no.	Parameter	Self organized intelligent multi time scale resource management
1	Computational time	Less
2	Efficiency	High
3	Reliability	High

6 Conclusion

In this paper, A Novel SDN-Based IoT Security Architecture Model for Big Data was implemented. The main intent of Novel Software-Defined Networking (SDN) is used to control and manage the network. Novel SDN controller protocol controls the devices linearly and in the same way to modify the protocol for improving the performance. Hence in this Novel SDN controller protocol there will be reduction of computational time and improvement of efficiency and reliability.

References

1. Gkioulos, V., Gunleifsen, H., Weldehawaryat, G.K.: A systematic literature review on military software defined networks. Fut. Internet **10**, 88 (2019). https://doi.org/10.3390/fi10090088
2. Kreutz, D., Ramos, F.M.V., Verissimo, P., Rothenberg, E., Azodolmolky, S., Uhlig, S.: Software-defined networking: a comprehensive survey. Manuscript received 31 May 2018
3. Braun, W., Menth, M.: Software-defined networking using OpenFlow: protocols, applications and architectural design choices. Fut. Internet **6**, 302–336 (2018). https://doi.org/10.3390/fi6 020302
4. Kamal, A.: Software-defined networking (SDN): a survey. Published online 7 February 2013 in Wiley Online Library
5. Ben Mamoun, M., Benaini, R.: An overview on SDN architectures with multiple controllers. J. Comput. Netw. Commun. **2016**(2), 1–8 (2016)
6. Quincozes, S.E., Soares, A.A.Z., Oliveira, W., Cordeiro, E.B.: Survey and comparison of SDN controllers for tele protection and control power systems. IFIP (2017). ISBN 978-3-903176-23-2
7. Mckeown, V., Mancuso, V., Banchs, A., Zaks, S., Capone, A.: Enhanced content update dissemination through D2D in 5G cellular networks. IEEE Trans. Wirel. Commun. **15**(11), 7517–7530 (2016)
8. Kim, Feamster: Principles and Practices for Securing Software-Defined Networks. ONF TR-511 (January 2016)
9. Hakiri, A., Gokhalec, A., Berthoua, P., Schmidtc, D.C., Thierrya, G.: Software-defined networking: challenges and research opportunities for future internet. Comput. Netw. **75**(Part A), 453–471 (2014)
10. Gude, Pedreiras, P., Fonseca, P., Almeida, L.: On the adequacy of SDN and TSN for Industry. CISTER Research Center (2015)
11. Liu, G., Yu, F.R., Ji, H., Leung, V.C., Li, X.: In-band full-duplex relaying for 5G cellular networks with wireless virtualization. IEEE Netw. **29**(6), 54–61 (2015)
12. Qiao, J., Shen, X.S., Mark, J.W., Shen, Q., He, Y., Lei, L.: Enabling device-to-device communications in millimeter-wave 5G cellular networks. IEEE Commun. Mag. **53**(1), 209–215 (2015)
13. Zakrzewska, A., Ruepp, S., Berger, M.S.: Towards converged 5G mobile networks-challenges and current trends (June 2014)
14. Sulyman, A.I., Nassar, A.T., Samimi, M.K., MacCartney, G.R., Rappaport, T.S., Alsanie, A.: Radio propagation path loss models for 5G cellular networks in the 28 GHz and 38 GHz millimeter-wave bands. IEEE Commun. Mag. **52**(9), 78–86 (2014)

Cloud Effects on Organisational Performance: A Local Government Perspective

Prasanna Balasooriya$^{(\boxtimes)}$ ⓘ, Santoso Wibowo ⓘ, Marilyn Wells ⓘ, and Steven Gordon ⓘ

Central Queensland University, Melbourne, Australia
p.balasooriya@cqu.edu.au

Abstract. The Cloud technology has been recognized as a potential technology which could be used to gain extra benefits to all levels of organisations including local government. It is also being found that successful adoption and use of the technology could improve the performance of organisation at various levels, but organisational performance also depends on various technical elements. Therefore, to investigate how successful adoption of Cloud technology and its use to gain higher level of performance, an integrated framework has been introduced by incorporating TOE and RBV theoretical frameworks together. Thus, the integrated conceptual framework proposed in this study will assist organisations to identify the key elements which are impacting the use of the Cloud technology. Similarly, the proposed framework will assist organisations to measure how Cloud technology could impact the "Business performance". This paper also suggested to develop a quantitative survey questionnaire which has all the required components derived from TOE and RBV frameworks. Survey will be distributed among the IT professionals who works in local government organisations across Australia and expected to have minimum of 400 responses to conduct an analysis. Both IBM SPSS and Smart PLS software applications will be used in this study. In addition, two-tier structural equation modelling technique will be used to assess the results. Lastly, the findings of this research study are expected to add a new knowledge to the IS literature and a proposed framework will be a useful guideline for organisation to assess their capabilities in use of Cloud technology.

Keywords: Local government · TOE · RBV · Cloud use · Organisational performance

1 Introduction

The cloud technology has defined as "The National Institute of Standards and Technology (NIST) defines Cloud technology as a model for enabling convenient, on-demand network access to a shared pool of configurable computing resources including networks, servers, storage, applications, and services that can be rapidly provisioned and released with minimal management effort or service provider interaction" [1] Thus, Cloud technology has been recognized by previous studies as an "innovative" technology, which could potentially effects the organisational performance [2]. In addition, Cloud will offer

© Springer Nature Singapore Pte Ltd. 2022
S. R. Pokhrel et al. (Eds.): ATIS 2021, CCIS 1554, pp. 149–156, 2022.
https://doi.org/10.1007/978-981-19-1166-8_12

"reduce cost, improve performance, reduce maintenance, better storage, and increased security" as an additional capability, which organisations could use to maximize their performance [3]. Thus, irrespective of the services, benefits or the sector of the organisation fits in, Cloud has recognized for its value creation. Therefore, "it is important to understand" the issues surrounding cloud adoption and its potential on the organization's performance. As suggested by Chinyao et al. [4], it is worth to investigate the post-adoption of the Cloud to measure how technology has improved organisational performance rather investigating pre-adoption concerns.

This research study has identified two main research gaps as (i) even though the convincing previous literature in the area of Cloud adoption and security, there are limited research has been found focusing Cloud usage & Cloud effects, and (ii). Organisational performance. As most of the existing literature focused on either Cloud adoption or pre-adoption processes, there were limited attention on the "post-adoption" implications on organisations. Thus, this research study is expected address the post-adoption of Cloud including cloud usage, effects and organisation performances [5, 4].

Therefore, to fulfill the gaps identified above, this study will attempt to answer the following research questions: (i) exploration of an integrated framework to explore the use of Cloud technology (ii). Identification of key elements which could influence the use of Cloud and organisational performance. Thus, this research study is expected to integrate two theoretical frameworks together to provide a comprehensive view of post-implementation impacts of Cloud technology. In this paper, researchers have proposed to integrate Technology, Organisation and Environment (TOE) and Resource-Based View (RBV) theories to provide a complete understanding of the post-adoption stages and successes. Thereafter, develops a new theoretical framework based on the existing studies and literature illustrated in Table 1 which will be a useful resource to assess post-adoption impacts in the future. Furthermore, the findings of this research will be used to gain an understanding of the Cloud usage and its effects on organisational performance. Furthermore, it is important to determine how use of Cloud could "affects organisational growth, performance and business values" [6].

This paper is therefore organised into five sections as follows; Sect. 1 starts with the introduction, Sect. 2 which will discuss the existing literature on TOE and RBV. Section 3 will be used to discuss the research model and hypothesis which are related to this study. Section 4 will present the proposed methodology and future work followed by Sect. 5, which will present the expected outcome of the study.

2 Literature Review

2.1 Technology, Organization and Environment (TOE) Framework

The TOE framework has been extensively used by many organisations to explore the technical factors which are influencing new technology adoptions. The TOE framework comprises three major contexts namely technology (T), organisation (O) and environment (E) [7]. Thus, many researchers in the past and present have use TOE framework to access the factors which are influential on new technology adoption [5]. Therefore, the influential factors derived from TOE is expected to be used to access the technological influence and Resources Based View theory will be used to measure the performances gained by adopting the new technology such as Cloud.

2.2 Resource-Based View (RBV) Theory

The resources-based view theory initially used in the field of strategic management. The RBV theoretical framework will assist organisations to explore how organisational performance will depends on the "organisational resources & capabilities" which are hard to replace easily [8]. As Clemons et al., [9] and Powel et al., [10] believe, organisation could gain higher performance from new technology resources when they "embedded in a way where it produces valuable and sustainable resource". Wegloop [11] noted that "internal resources and capabilities" could influence the organisational "strategy and behaviour". Thus, this will allow organisations to deploy their invaluable resources strategically to gain higher performance as they expect [12]. Therefore, once organisational resources deployed strategically, it will assist organisation to improve the organisational "efficiency and effectiveness" which could leads to gain higher performance [13]. Kozlenkova et al. [12] also believe that only the resources which are "valuable, rare and inimitable" can provide the "competitive advantage" against others in the field. Therefore, in conclusion, RBV is a valuable theoretical framework which can be used as a "guideline" for organisation to assess their use of "resources and performance" [14].

Therefore, in this research study, the researchers are expected integrate RBV and TOE framework together to provide an integrative view to fulfill the gaps identified in the study. By incorporating to different theories together, the researchers will assist organisation to determine how organisational "resources and technical capabilities" could assist the organisation to improve their performances. Similarly, the previous literature such as [15] and [16] have used similar and incorporated framework in their studies in eBusiness and eCommerce.

3 Research Model and Hypothesis

As illustrated in Fig. 1, the proposed conceptual framework was developed by incorporating both TOE and RBV theories together. Thus, based on the factors identified in previous studies and illustrated in Table 1, Technical/Business resources, Organizational characteristics/change management and vendor support/legislative requirements will be discussed as part of the TOE framework. Thereafter, organisational performances will be discussed under RBV. In addition, size of the organisation, gender and education level have been used as a moderator variable which will be used to assess how those will impact technical, organisation and environment capabilities against the Cloud usage. Also, moderator variable size and management support will be used to assess how those variables are impacting the performance.

3.1 Technical Capacity

The organisations technical capacity describes the organisations "hardware, software and network capabilities". Thus, these capabilities will assist the organisation to adopt Cloud technology and use it as an emerging technology [17, 18]. Hence, the technical capability of the organisation could assist them gaining a "competitive advantage" against other organisations in the same industry.

3.2 Business Resources

The organisations business resources play an important role in technology adoption by organizing the business resources and building "business relationships" including "vendors, suppliers and arranging training, financial resources" for successful implementation and use of the technology [19, 10]. Thus, hypothesis 2 (H2) has created to test how business resources could influence the Cloud usage.

Hypothesis 1 has been developed to test how "technology capacity" will influence the "Cloud usages" in the organisation.

Hypothesis 1: Technical capacity of the organisation will positively influence the "Cloud use".

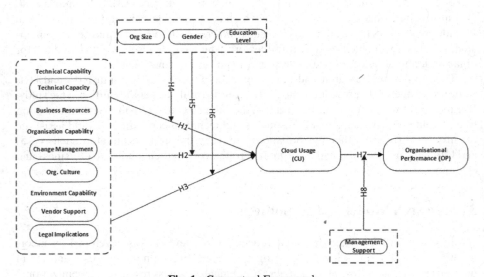

Fig. 1. Conceptual Framework

3.3 Change Management

The change management process is a key element of an organisation during the adoption of the new technologies such as "Cloud adoption". Thus, this element will define how well new technology will "fit" with the existing "business processes" and how well users will accept the technology [20, 21].

Table 1. Summary of the previous literature focused on TOE-RBV

Framework	Factors	References
Technology (T)	Technical resources	[17, 18]
	Business resources	[19, 10]
Organisation (O)	Org. characterizes/culture	[27, 28]
	Change management	[21, 20]
Environment (E)	Vendor support	[24, 25]
	Legal/legislative support	[25, 26]
RBV	Business performance	[8, 9, 10]

3.4 Organisational Characteristics

When organisations demonstrate positive culture for adoption of new technologies such as Cloud, organisation can implement them successfully with the support of all levels of employees. In addition, the positive culture will encourage employees to use Cloud as a potential technology which could enhance their productivity and efficiently [22, 23].

Thus, hypothesis 2 below has been created to test the organisational specific characteristics such as change management and culture impact the Cloud use.

Hypothesis 2: Organisational capacity will positively impact the "Cloud use".

3.5 Vendor Support

In new technology adoption, vendor support has been recognized as a critical element. Creating a positive vendor relationship also will organisation to develop a positive relation between vendor and the organisation which could see as a factor for successful adoption and implementation of the technology. The successful relationship includes the positive responses and assistance they provide for the organisation and continues training of the technology [24, 25].

3.6 Legal/Policy Implication

The legal and legislative policy support is a key factor that could influence local government organisations to adopt and use new technologies such as Cloud. When there is a clear and supportive legal framework is established, it will encourage organisations to adopt the technologies without any hesitation. In addition, the legal and policy framework must cover the demanding issues such as "security, privacy and data confidentiality" [25, 26].

Hypothesis 3: A supporting legal framework will positively encourage organisations to use Cloud.

3.7 Business Performance

The goal of adopting a new technology like Cloud is to provide a competitive advantage and gain maximum performance by reducing/removing the waste. This goal can be achieved in various ways like reduction of cost, maximizing the technical resources used, increasing efficiency of the process etc., and Cloud technology is best suited solution for it [8, 9, 10].

Hypothesis 4: Successful use of Cloud will positively impact to gain higher performance.

In addition, size of the organisation, Management support, knowledge and experience have been used as moderating elements, and researcher believes that those elements could also influence the use of cloud as an emerging technology.

4 Proposed Methodology and Future Work

The main aim of this research study is to explore how Cloud technology will impact organisational performance in local government environment. Thus, ultimate aim of this study will be achieved by using an integrated framework developed on the foundations of Technology, Organisation and Environment (TOE) framework and Resourced based view (RBV) theory. As previous literature suggests, this study will be adopting a quantitative research methodology where it will be used to test the conceptual framework and hypothesis. The target audience for the quantitative survey questionnaire will be the Information Technology professionals and middle/senior level management staff who will be working in local government environment across Australia. These audiences are expected to be an expert in their area and have depth understanding of the operations of information technology and strategic management.

The survey questionnaire will be developed and distributed to all the local government employees who worked in information Technology area across Australia and expected to collect at least 300–400 responses. The expected survey questionnaire will include three major components as (i) collection of demographic information such as gender, organisation size and respondent's education qualification. (ii). Collection of technical information, which was derived from TOE framework, and (iii). Information about organisational performance. Thereafter, both IBM SPSS and SmartPLS software applications will be used to analysis the data. A two-tier approach will be used as part of structural equation modelling techniques, which allows to assess both (a) factor analysis and (b) structural equation model.

5 Expected Contribution

The main aim of this research study is to assess how organisational capabilities could influence the Cloud use, and how successful use of could help local government organisation to gain better performance. Thus, the key findings of this study will contribute to the existing theory, which will be a useful material for future researchers. On other side, the newly developed framework will practically help local government organisations to determine which factors are more important to encourage the use of Cloud and how those will help to gain better performances.

References

1. Mell, P., Grance, T.: SP 800–145. The NIST Definition of Cloud Computing: Recommendations of the National Institute of Standards and Technology. NIST Special Publication (2011)
2. Balasooriya, P.: A Confirmatory investigation of the factors influencing the cloud adoption in local government organisations in Australia. In: Proceedings of the 29th Australasian Conference on Information Systems, University of Sydney, Australia, pp.1–12(2018)
3. Maresova, P., Sobeslav, V., Krejcar, O.: Cost–benefit analysis – evaluation model of Cloud computing deployment for use in companies. Appl. Econ. 49(6), 521–533 (2017)
4. Chinyao, L., Yahsueh, C., Mingchang, W.: Understanding the determinants of cloud computing adoption. Ind. Manage. Data Syst. 111(7), 1006–1023 (2011)
5. Gangwar, H., Ramaswamy, H.: Understanding determinants of cloud computing adoption using an integrated TAM-TOE model. J. Enterp. Inf. Manage. 28(1), 107–130 (2015)
6. Ravichandran, T., Lertwongsatien, C.: Effect of information systems resources and abilities on firm performance. J. Manage. Inf. Syst. 21(4), 237–276 (2005)
7. Gutierrez, A., Boukrami, E., Lumsden, R.: Technological, organisational and environmental factors influencing managers' decision to adopt cloud computing in the UK. J. Enterp. Inf. Manage. 28(6), 788–807 (2015)
8. Bruque, S., Moyano, J., Maqueira, J.: Cloud computing, Web 2.0, and operational performance. Int. J. Logist. Manage. 26(3), 426–458 (2015)
9. Clemons, E., Row, M.: Sustaining IT advantage: the role of structural differences. MIS Q. 15(3), 275–294 (1991)
10. Powell, C., Dent-Micallef, A.: Information technology as competitive advantage: the role of human, business and technology resources. Strateg. Manage. J. 18(5), 375–405 (1997)
11. Wegloop, P.: Linking firm strategy and government action: towards a resource-based perspective on innovation and technology policy. Technol. Soc. 17(4), 413–428 (1995)
12. Kozlenkova, V., Samaha, A., Palmatier, R.W.: Resource-based theory in marketing. J. Acad. Mark. Sci. 42(1), 1–21 (2014)
13. Wernerfelt, B.: A resource-based view of the firm. Strateg. Manage. 5(2), 171–180 (1984)
14. Lee, G., Kwak, H.: An open government maturity model for social media based public engagement. Gov. Inf. Q. 29(4), 492–503 (2012)
15. Mohamed, I., Marthandan, G., Norzaidi, M., Chong, S.: E-commerce usage and business performance in the Malaysian tourism sector: Empirical analysis. Inf. Manage. Comput. Secur. 17(1), 166–185 (2009)
16. Zhu, K., Kraemer, K.: Post-adoption variations in usage and value of e-business by organizations: cross-country evidence from the retail industry. Inf. Syst. Res. 16(1), 61–84 (2005)
17. Chuang, S.: A resource-based perspective on knowledge management capability and competitive advantage: an empirical investigation. Exp. Syst. Appl. 27(1), 459–465 (2004)
18. Teo, S., Ranganathan, C.: Leveraging IT resources and capabilities at the housing and development board. J. Strateg. Inf. Syst. 12(1), 229–249 (2003)
19. Molla, A., Licker, P.: Perceived e-readiness factors in e-commerce adoption: an empirical investigation in a developing country. Int. J. Electron. Commer. 10(1), 83–110 (2005)
20. Kuan, K., Chau, P.: A perception-based model for EDI adoption in small businesses using a technology organization-environment framework. Inf. Manage. 38(1), 507–521 (2001)
21. Kim, G., Shin, B., Kim, K., Lee, H.: IT capabilities, process-oriented dynamic capabilities, and firm financial performance. J. Assoc. Inf. Syst. 12(1), 487–517 (2011)
22. Ke, W., Wei, K.: Organizational culture and leadership in ERP implementation. In: Pacific Asia Conference on Information Systems (2005)

23. Nguyen, T.: Information technology adoption in SMEs: an integrated framework. Int. J. Entrep. Behav. Res. **15**(1), 162–186 (2009)
24. Ismail, I., Abdullah, H., Shamsudin, A., Ariffin, N.: Implementation differences of Hospital Information System (HIS) in Malaysian public hospitals. Int. J. Soc. Sci. Humanit. **20**(21), 22–29 (2013)
25. Chang, I., Hwang, G., Hung, C., Lin, H., Yen, C.: Factors affecting the adoption of electronic signature: executives' perspective of hospital information department. Decis. Support Syst. **44**, 350–359 (2007)
26. Lian, W., Yen, C., Wang, T.: An exploratory study to understand the critical factors affecting the decision to adopt cloud computing in Taiwan hospital. Int. J. Inf. Manage. **34**(1), 28–36 (2014)
27. Livari, J., Huisman, M.: The relationship between organizational culture and the deployment of systems development methodologies. MIS Q. **31**(1), 35–58 (2007)
28. Akman, I., Yazici, A., Mishra, A., Arifoglu, A.: E-government: a global view and an empirical evaluation of some attributes of citizens. Gov. Inf. Q. **22**(2), 239–257 (2005)

Communication and Data Mining

RTOS Based Embedded Solution for Multi-purpose Radio Frequency Communication

Meghang Nagavekar[1] ⓘ, Arthur Gomes[2] ⓘ, and Srikanth Prabhu[3](✉) ⓘ

[1] Department of Electronics and Instrumentation, Manipal Institute of Technology, Manipal, Karnataka, India
[2] Department of Mechatronics Engineering, Manipal Institute of Technology, Manipal, Karnataka, India
[3] Department of Computer Science and Engineering, Manipal Institute of Technology, Manipal, Karnataka, India
srikanth.prabhu@manipal.edu

Abstract. Based on Real-Time Operating System (RTOS) concepts, a continuous data transceiver system is designed. The wireless data transmission is enabled using the HC-12 board as a Radio Frequency (Bluetooth) module. To achieve computations for data/signal processing, an STM32 microcontroller is chosen. An open-source Middleware—FreeRTOS is used for implementing RTOS in the microcontroller. The complete transceiver system consists of an electronic remote controller as the transmitter and a multi-purpose electronic driver setup as a receiver. The receiver module can be integrated into various systems as per the user's requirements. The controller's application in future research prospects ranges from the manual operation of industrial machinery to the safety testing/prototyping of medical robots. The overall system is fast, reliable and convenient.

Keywords: Embedded systems · Radio frequency · Bluetooth · FreeRTOS · STM32

1 Introduction

The demand for automation in various sectors of the industry is growing rapidly. Industrial automation protocols cannot be implemented directly without thorough testing. Hence, manual operation of machinery in its initial stages of development or for prototyping is an integral part of testing software, internal hardware, or structural analysis of mechanical systems [1]. A Universal, multi-purpose, wireless controller can be used for a wide variety of testing protocols. This paper presents a design of a wireless controller that is easy to use and can be interfaced with multiple control systems and I/O devices.

Current Industrial controllers involve interfacing hardware to PLCs (programmable logic controllers), PACs (programmable automation controllers), DCSs (distributed control system), RTUs (remote terminal units), etc. These controllers are built for manufacturing assembly lines and any function that requires high-reliability control or process

© Springer Nature Singapore Pte Ltd. 2022
S. R. Pokhrel et al. (Eds.): ATIS 2021, CCIS 1554, pp. 159–171, 2022.
https://doi.org/10.1007/978-981-19-1166-8_13

fault diagnosis. These devices are specifically designed and rigorously tested to ensure they can withstand operating in an industrial environment where they may be exposed to shocks, vibration, noise, corrosive materials and extreme temperature fluctuations [2]. Although PLCs are robust, there are highly application-specific and not general purpose. They can alter process control systems based on predefined automated conditions. Microcontroller-based controllers can be programmed easily to handle computationally intensive tasks and complex communication protocols. Microcontroller based controllers can achieve long-distance remote data transceiving while industry logic controllers require a lot of hardware setup for the same. For fast prototyping and testing, microcontroller-based controllers are cheap and convenient. Hence, the following design of a microcontroller-based system provides the user complete customizability and transparency about the underlying processes.

An STM32F103C8-T6 microcontroller is chosen as the main control device for its low power usage, small size, and comparatively higher clock frequency. STM32 is a 32-bit microcontroller family based on ARM Cortex-M3 CPU architecture and is developed by STMicroelectronics. [3] The STM32-F1xx series is a Medium Density Performance controller chip with 64 KB of flash memory and 20 KB of RAM size. It has 42 GPIO pins with 2 APB buses for I/O interfacing, a high-speed 8 MHz crystal oscillator that has an internal PLL for a possible clock frequency of 72 MHz. It is programmed and debugged using a ST-Link bootloader device that is easy to use. Separate data and power pins are provided on the microcontroller board for the programmer to be connected as shown in Fig. 1. The microcontroller is best suited for its fast response speeds, available hardware resources, better developer community support, and comparatively larger I/O interface density. More information about this microcontroller can be taken from the datasheet.

Fig. 1. An STM32F103C8 microcontroller board

The transmitter and receiver both incorporate the HC-12 Bluetooth module to enable continuous radio frequency communication. The module operates on a 433 MHz to 473 MHz frequency band and can work under a total of 100 channels.

Attaching an antenna to the HC-12 module extends the transmission range to around 2 km. The maximum transmitting power is around 100 mW. This module is chosen for its long-range and easy-to-use capabilities [3]. More information about this module can be taken from the datasheet.

The microcontroller firmware has FreeRTOS drivers. RTOS makes the transceiver system more efficient by enabling smart task-scheduling. Generic microcontroller firmware sequentially executes tasks whereas RTOS uses priority-based task management by using interrupts in real-time [4]. Involving real time task-scheduling guarantees signal processing and transmission within the articulated time constraints without the other microcontroller-based hardware resources interfering. Data packaging, signal processing, timer control and UART transmission are hence able to work independently.

2   Preliminaries

The complete system consists of two modules—The Controller module and the Interface module. The complete circuit interface is shown in Fig. 2 and is explained below.

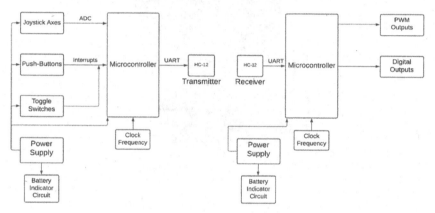

Fig. 2. Complete circuit interface

2.1   Controller Module

The controller module is an intuitive, manually operated device consisting of two dual-axis joysticks for analog data, twelve push-buttons and two toggle switches for digital data and one HC-12 Bluetooth module for wireless transmission of data to the interface module. The complete microcontroller connection for the controller module is made as shown in Fig. 6.

Joysticks
The joysticks are interfaced with the microcontroller using an analog to digital converter (ADC) [5]. The STM32F103C8 has a 4-channel 12-bit ADC which is connected to the APB2 bus. The ADC of the microcontroller works at a maximum frequency of 14 MHz. The individual axes of each joystick are connected to its corresponding ADC channel [6]. The ADC cannot compute the values of each channel simultaneously. Hence, a DMA (direct memory access) is used to store the values computed by each channel of ADC

until all channel values are computed. The individual values are stored in a 1-D array and can be read easily. The microcontroller can compute ADC values for voltages between 2.4 V and 3.6 V. Hence a voltage divider will be used to scale the potential to the required range. The ADC in this microcontroller is set up to be used in Continuous Conversion Mode. In Continuous Conversion Mode, the analog data is continually converted and written to the ADC data registers. Data from the previous conversion is overwritten regardless of whether the data has been read or not.

By using this method, an accurate real-time digital conversion is possible, and hence, the latency between the joystick actual value and the computed value is reduced. The connections with the joysticks are made as shown in Fig. 3.

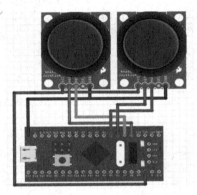

Fig. 3. Joystick module interface

Push-Buttons

The pushbuttons are directly connected to the GPIO pins of the microcontroller. The corresponding GPIO pins are set up in input mode. When a push-button is pressed, the corresponding GPIO pins experience a voltage and will read it as a digital "HIGH". The toggle switches are connected in a similar manner. These interfaces work as external interrupts that can be triggered inside the RTOS kernel. The connections with the pushbutton are made as shown in Fig. 4.

Battery-Indicator

The power supply of the controller is given by four AA batteries. If the total battery voltage falls below a certain level, the HC-12 and the controller ceases to work. Hence, a battery indicator circuit is designed. An LM3914 IC is used with a LED strip to indicate the battery potential. This IC uses a series of Op-Amps as comparators to divide their circuit into multiple potential nodes. When potential at a node goes below a threshold voltage, the node reaches a logic "LOW". Since this circuit consumes a lot of power, it cannot be powered continuously.

Hence, a switch is used to switch ON this circuit whenever the user wants to see the indication. For more information about this IC, refer to its datasheet. The connections with the power supply are made as shown in Fig. 5.

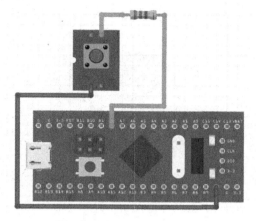

Fig. 4. Push-button interface

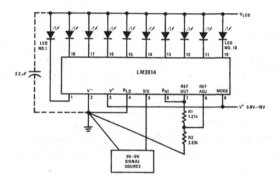

Fig. 5. Battery indicator circuit

Transmitter Module

The HC-12 Bluetooth module connected to the STM32 microcontroller works as a wireless data transmitter module. Communication between the Bluetooth module and the microcontroller is executed by a protocol known as Universal Asynchronous receiver-transmitter protocol or UART.

This communication protocol involves a two-wire logic signal connection (TX and RX) between transmitter and receiver [7]. The RX pin of the microcontroller is connected to the TX pin of the HC-12 module and the TX pin of the microcontroller is connected to the RX pin of the HC-12 module.

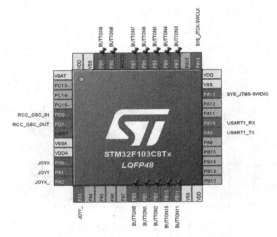

Fig. 6. Microcontroller connections for controller module

2.2 Interface Module

The interface module is a board having several output connections. The whole board is intended to be placed on the application-specific machinery. This module has the following connections as shown in Fig. 7.

Pulse Width Modulated Outputs

The PWM ports will output pulse signals, each having a certain duty cycle generated by a 12-bit resolution timer. The duty cycle depends on the output generated by the

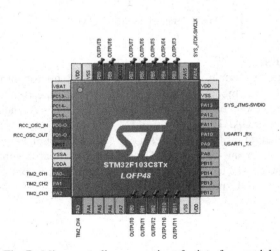

Fig. 7. Microcontroller connections for interface module

Joystick axes on the controller module. The duty cycle will change when the joystick values change. There will be four ports for PWM output on the interface module.

Digital Outputs

There are twelve digital outputs on the interface module, each corresponding to a push-button/toggle switch on the controller module.

These outputs represent the state of the digital inputs on the controller module. When a push-button is pressed on the controller, a logical "HIGH" is written to the respective output on the interface module. This data can be used to sequence specific actuations or switching ON or OFF certain devices like sensors and indicators.

Receiver Module

The HC-12 module works as a receiver in this system. It is wired to the microcontroller in the same way as in the controller module. Figure 7 represents connections made in the interface module.

3 Algorithm

The microcontrollers perform most of the logical and computational tasks in this system. The whole system is designed to operate with least possible computational complexity and is also capable of performing several tasks simultaneously. This is achieved by creating the RTOS kernel inside the main firmware using FreeRTOS drivers and libraries. The initial stage of defining basic functions is by initializing individual hardware resources such as Timers, ADCs, Interrupts, RTCs (Real Time Clock) and UART drivers before configuring the RTOS tasks. The data packaging part of the algorithm is designed taking into consideration the data width of UART and is by far the most efficient way of communication. The following are the stages in which the firmware is designed.

3.1 Controller Module

System Clock Configuration

The main clock signal for the microcontroller is provided by the 8 MHz crystal oscillator that is connected to the HSE (High-speed clock) interface of the microcontroller. This clock signal is passed into a PLL (Phase Locked Loop) that scales the input clock frequency to 72 MHz. This clock frequency is passed to individual APB Buses and ADCs. The APB buses work at 72 MHz whereas the ADCs clock input is pre-scaled to work at 12 MHz. (The ADCs work at a maximum clock frequency of 14 MHz.) The clock configuration in the microcontroller is done as shown in Fig. 8.

Hardware Resources Configuration

HAL (Hardware Abstraction Layer) libraries are used for the working of ADCs, UART communication, push-buttons, and for generating PWM signals. The HAL drivers are low-level drivers that help avoid general bare-metal programming and saves time while debugging the firmware. The first step is initializing the hardware resources using the

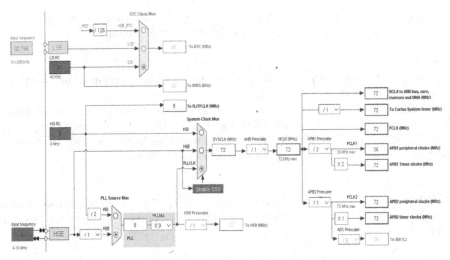

Fig. 8. Microcontroller system clock configuration (STM32 CubeIDE)

HAL libraries. The call-back functions for the corresponding hardware components are then created.

RTOS Kernel

The RTOS function handles are created automatically by the FreeRTOS middleware [4, [8]. A total of 5 tasks are created for the efficient working of the system as shown in Fig. 9. The first four tasks are dedicated to fetch/update the ADC values from their respective joystick axes.

The fifth task is for detecting push button presses in real-time. This task requires external interrupts to be called. All tasks will run simultaneously using smart task scheduling techniques.

```
osThreadDef(ADC0, ADC0Func, osPriorityNormal, 0, 128);
ADC0Handle = osThreadCreate(osThread(ADC0), NULL);

osThreadDef(ADC1, ADC1Func, osPriorityNormal, 0, 128);
ADC1Handle = osThreadCreate(osThread(ADC1), NULL);

osThreadDef(ADC2, ADC2Func, osPriorityNormal, 0, 128);
ADC2Handle = osThreadCreate(osThread(ADC2), NULL);

osThreadDef(ADC3, ADC3Func, osPriorityNormal, 0, 128);
ADC3Handle = osThreadCreate(osThread(ADC3), NULL);

osThreadDef(PushButtons, PushButtonsFunc, osPriorityNormal, 0, 128);
PushButtonsHandle = osThreadCreate(osThread(PushButtons), NULL);
```

Fig. 9. RTOS kernel initialization

Data Packaging
Data Packaging is the most important part of this system. The computed values of all used hardware resources are updated in a global variable after every task iteration. The global variable is an unsigned 64-bit integer that is available to be modified by all working tasks.

UART Transmission
Since UART communication transmits only 8-bit data packets, the 64-bit unsigned integer variable is broken into 16 divisions (each having 4-bits from the variable) as shown in Fig. 10. Each division requires 4 identifier bits. Hence, the data to be transmitted consists of sixteen 8-bit numbers. These 8-bit numbers will be sent continuously to the HC-12 module to be transmitted to the receiver module wirelessly.

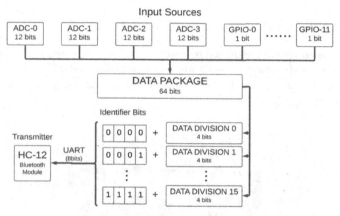

Fig. 10. Data packaging in controller module

3.2 Interface Module

The system clock and hardware resources configurations performed are identical to the transmitter module. The microcontroller on the receiver side is interfaced with the HC-12 that receives data using UART. The ring buffer interrupt method is used by the microcontroller to update the UART receive buffer variable whenever the data is received as shown in Fig. 11. These individual packages have the data of individual ADC and digital values. This data is converted to Pulse Width Modulated values (imitating the ADC values on the controller module) and digital values (imitating the push-buttons on the controller module).

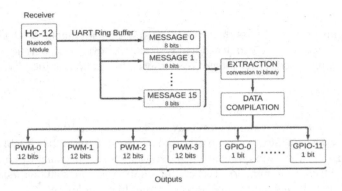

Fig. 11. Data packaging in interface module

4 Results and Inferences

A set of experiments were conducted to ensure the proper working of the system. The main aim of these experiments was to observe waveforms of the UART signals and to test the endurance of the system for calculating the power consumption. The experiment setup is shown in Fig. 12.

Fig. 12. Experimental setup

A National Instruments Elvis II model is used for providing a variable potential supply and a digital waveform logic analyzer to observe the UART signals. The variable potential mimics the joystick axes and hence is connected to the ADC of the microcontroller. The UART pins are connected to the oscilloscope ports to observe the waveforms. The Fig. 13 shows the UART waveforms observed under an oscilloscope. The image concludes that the waveform is unaltered by the simultaneous working of the ADC as well as internal computations. In the interface module, the PWM outputs are not affected by the simultaneous receiving of UART signals. The interrupt service routine used by the real time operating systems manages the tasks with no data leaks and errors even at maximum operating frequency of the microcontroller. Hence, RTOS is responsible for handling tasks with high reliability.

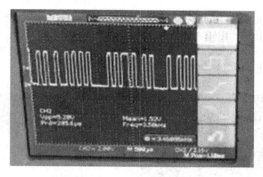

Fig. 13. UART waveform output

Conventional industrial controllers do not have wireless data transmission techniques. They rely on their custom wired s-bus protocols for inter-system communication. This proposed controller system introduces a programmable method of wireless communication.

Comparison between microcontrollers was conducted. It was concluded that the system does not have any demanding requirements from a microcontroller except that the system should run on comparatively higher clock frequency and have a good measure of hardware resources. The STM32F103C8 satisfies all these requirements.

One prominent drawback of the system is the high and continuous consumption of power. The high frequency PLL and the battery indicator circuit consume most of the power. One more drawback of the system is the complex user debugging that involves interfacing more devices as per usage and its programming. These issues can be rectified further by improving the structure of the algorithm for general usage as well as by involving multi conditional algorithms for "sleep mode" to save power.

5   Applications and Future Scope

This module has a wide variety of application in the field of Industrial Automation, Robot Prototyping, Surgical and Aerial Robotics, Construction Equipment and any other application that requires very precise and real-time user control of actuators and peripherals with least possible latency. A few such examples are listed below.

5.1   Robotic Arm

This system is implemented to actuate a seven degrees of freedom (7-dof) Robotic Arm. The controller is used to manually operate joints and control end-effector position using inverse kinematic solvers [5, 9]. The interface module is placed on the base of the Robotic Arm and connected directly to the actuator drivers. Using combinations of the digital and PWM outputs, each required joint can be moved with precision and minimum latency. It is implemented in a visualization software—Rviz in a ROS (Robot Operating System) environment as shown in Fig. 14. For the movement of individual joints, multiple nodes communicate in the ROS environment. Figure 14 represents how joints can be manipulated using a "joint_state_publisher" node. The node then reads values from the controller (interface module) that is connected to the ROS environment using a serial communication node "ros_serial". The robot used in the simulation is a standard KUKA 7-dof robotic arm.

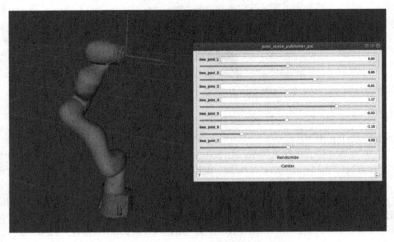

Fig. 14. KUKA robotic arm simulation

5.2 Drone Control

This device can be used as a general-purpose drone controller. Due to its programmable configurations, the interface module can be connected to the flight controller input for any kind of drone design.

It can also help in optimizing drone flight control firmware by interfacing this system with SITL (Software in the Loop) simulation environment for testing. Using custom programmable sequences of digital inputs (push-buttons), the drone can perform specific autonomous tasks and motions.

5.3 Multi "Slave" Interface Devices

Multiple interface modules can act like slave modules (the controller module being the master) in order to increase the number of total output interfaces in the system. All the Bluetooth modules present in the system should be configured to work on the same bandwidth. To send exclusive data to individual slave modules, the unused bits of the data package variable can be used as identifier bits.

6 Conclusions

This paper represents design of a microcontroller based industrial grade wireless controller. The microcontroller is programmed using an RTOS kernel. The advantages associated with RTOS kernels are low data processing and transmission latency and comparatively lower power consumption than generic microcontroller firmware.

This system was initially implemented on actuators like servo and stepper motors. Interfacing complex transducer involving control loops with this system guarantees responsive behavior with very high precision. Prospective applications of this system include testing articulated Robotic Arms employed in industrial assembly lines, premature development and prototyping of unmanned aerial vehicles and simple DIY projects.

References

1. Yu, C., Ma, X., Fang, F., Qian, K., Yao, S., Zou, Y.: Design of controller system for industrial robot based on RTOS Xenomai. In: 2017 12th IEEE Conference on Industrial Electronics and Applications (ICIEA), pp. 221–226. IEEE, June 2017
2. Su, K.M., Liu, I.H., Li, J.S.: The risk of industrial control system programmable logic controller default configurations. In: 2020 International Computer Symposium (ICS), pp. 443–447. IEEE, December 2020
3. Singh, V.K., Sahu, A., Beg, A., Khan, B., Kumar, S.: Speed & direction control of DC motor through Bluetooth HC-05 using Arduino. In: 2018 International Conference on Advanced Computation and Telecommunication (ICACAT), pp. 1–3. IEEE, December 2018
4. Rajulu, B., Dasiga, S., Iyer, N.R.: Open source RTOS implementation for on-board computer (OBC) in STUDSAT-2. In: 2014 IEEE Aerospace Conference, pp. 1–13. IEEE, March 2014
5. Rahman, R., Rahman, M.S., Bhuiyan, J.R.: Joystick controlled industrial robotic system with robotic arm. In: 2019 IEEE International Conference on Robotics, Automation, Artificial-intelligence and Internet-of-Things (RAAICON), pp. 31–34. IEEE (2019)
6. Gong, Y., Zhang, P.: Design of curtain automatic control system based on STM32. In: 2020 2nd International Conference on Artificial Intelligence and Advanced Manufacture (AIAM), pp. 38–41. IEEE, October 2020
7. Agarwal, N., Reddy, S.N.: Design & development of daughter board for Raspberry Pi to support Bluetooth communication using UART. In: International Conference on Computing, Communication & Automation, pp. 949–954. IEEE, May 2015
8. Elsir, M.T., Sebastian, P., Yap, V.V.: A RTOS for educational purposes. In: 2010 International Conference on Intelligent and Advanced Systems, pp. 1–4. IEEE, June 2010
9. Agrawal, N.K., Singh, V.K., Parmar, V.S., Sharma, V.K., Singh, D., Agrawal, M.: Design and development of IoT based robotic arm by using Arduino. In: 2020 Fourth International Conference on Computing Methodologies and Communication (ICCMC), pp. 776–780. IEEE, March 2020

Author Index

Printed in the United States
by Baker & Taylor Publisher Services